Rebuilt, Not Broken

An Educator's Journey to

GREATNESS

Kelly Bullock Daugherty, Ed.D.

BSK PUBLISHING
Cleveland, Ohio

REBUILT, NOT BROKEN

Copyright © 2014 by Kelly Bullock Daugherty, Ed.D.

All rights reserved. No part of this book may be reproduced or transmitted in any form or by any means – electronic, mechanical, photocopying, recording, or otherwise - without prior written permission from the author, except in the case of brief quotations embodied in critical articles or reviews.

For more information on the author and Transitions Educational Consulting, LLC, visit **www.transitionseducates.com**

Edited by: M. White
Art Direction: Jacinda Walker
Designer & Photographer: Alaina Battle

Library of Congress Control Number: 2020923108

ISBN: 978-0-578-24420-4

Printed in United States of America

Acknowledgements

Without the encouragement of so many, this book would not be possible. Through my journey, my family has played an instrumental part in my growth and development. My parents, Steve and Doris Bullock, my brothers, Eric and Brian, my cousin Nicholas Kelly III, the entire Bullock and Daugherty Families, and many other cousins, nieces, and nephews, thank you for cheering me on behind the scenes in all my endeavors as I continued to strive to define my GREATNESS. Family is so very important to me and I appreciate your continuous love and support immensely.

I want to thank my husband, Leroy, and our three Blessings, Blair, Steven, and Kylee. You all are my reason for working so hard! I pray that in finding the GREATNESS in me, I have encouraged and motivated you to strive to find the GREATNESS in each of you! I am so proud to be your wife and mom. You push me to be my best and lift and support me when I feel I am not. Thank you for being a constant blessing in my life! I love you all to the moon and back!

Brian, you inspire and motivate me so much through all you do to be better. Thank you for always being my sounding board. With every conversation, you remind me of my worth and my inherent ability to impact change in my community and in the lives of those around me. You challenged me to get uncomfortable with being uncomfortable; to step outside of myself in order to be my BEST self. Thank you for your continuous love and support! You are an amazing model of excellence and scholarship. We have so much more to accomplish! #KeepGoing I love you!

Nicholas III (Tike), my cousin and best friend, I want to thank you for being a phone call away whenever I need you. You have helped me discover who I am as a person and a professional. You have reminded me that I can face the tallest and strongest of giants with the greatest of ease and skillful finesse. There are no words to express how much I appreciate your love and support! Thank you from the bottom of my heart! I love you MORE!

Harlan Jackson, my big brother and friend, I have known you and your family for many years; practically my entire life! As my brother's best friend, you have taken me in as your little sister. You have nurtured and loved me as if we were blood siblings, offering advice and support, and even a lecture or two here and there along my journey to define my GREATNESS. You push me to be more than I allow myself to be and that means so much. You are an inspiration and your words of motivation and encouragement mean so much to me. Thank you for being a blessing to my life! I love you so much!

Marva Bean White, you have supported every dream and every goal I have ever shared with you. You've prayed with me, for me, and continuously remind me that 'I can do ALL things through Christ who strengthens me' (Philippians 4:13). With all of my writing, you have been my second eyes. I appreciate that more than you could possibly know. Thank you for sharing my vision and for continuing to inspire and motivate me to do and be MORE.

To all the countless people who have challenged me, supported me, and cheered me on along my journey, I would not be the leader I am today if not for our interactions together, be it personally, professionally, or virtually. No matter our relationship, I have learned something from you and thank you for contributing to my life and my definition of GREATNESS.

Dedication

This book is dedicated to my family; my parents, my two older brothers, my husband and our 3 amazing Blessings who have kept me lifted, encouraged, and reminded that there is GREATER in me than I ever believed throughout my journey. I love you all to the moon and back!

I also dedicate this writing to Avery. Avery, you allowed me to see myself through you and charged me to do more for education without even knowing you had done so. Thank you for inciting me to remember the GREATNESS for teaching that was within me from the start because it pushed me to be a much better educator for students and teachers. I honor you with this book. Ubuntu (I am because you are).

Table of Contents

Acknowledgements... 3

Dedication... 5

Introduction.. 7

CHAPTER 1: Rebuilt, Not Broken............................... 11

CHAPTER 2: Growth Mindset.................................... 20

CHAPTER 3: Reinvent Yourself.................................. 32

CHAPTER 4: Empower 39

CHAPTER 5: Accountability....................................... 45

CHAPTER 6: Tenacity.. 53

CHAPTER 7: No Negativity.. 61

CHAPTER 8: Efficacy... 68

CHAPTER 9: Stay Focused... 77

CHAPTER 10: Success 82

Conclusion.. 86

References.. 91

Introduction

"What do you want to be when you grow up?" It's the age-old adage every child encounters at some point during their pubescent years. "It's never too early to begin thinking about it", my parents encouraged. My parents engaged me and my brothers in similar thought-provoking exchanges often. They spoke to us about our goals and the steps we would take to reach them.

Since the days of middle school, in the early 80s, I knew I wanted to work with young people. My friends would tell me that I always offered good advice, much like a psychologist. Building on what I knew was a strength I took a psychology class in high school and loved it. I knew that was what I would pursue as my major when I went to college.

There was no question that college was in my future. It was a clear expectation of my parents and of me. I wasn't the best student, but I got by. My first love was sports and I knew my grades had to be up to par in order to participate. I struggled with comprehension and advanced math classes. My teachers didn't expect much of me and as such, I didn't expect much of myself. Average grades were fine with me. It was the best I could do in my mind and if I could play sports, average was all I needed to be. My sports would get me to college.

Applying to several popular sports colleges would be an eye-opening wake up call. My grades and my test scores, while passing, would not be strong enough to keep up with the rigor and academic reputation of such colleges. It was discouraging to say the least. It turned out to be a blessing in disguise because I ended up having the best college experience anyone could ask for. I attended Virginia State University (VSU) in Petersburg, Virginia. It was at VSU that I realized my true academic potential. I did go on to study psychology and in my first semester, I earned straight A's. The head of the Psychology department was tough. She was stern and quite challenging. She was very intimidating in her approach, but it was a necessary approach for me. I realized later it was because she was pushing me to reach my full potential. I finally did reach my full potential, graduating with honors.

After graduation, I began working with cognitively and developmentally disabled children at a residential facility in my area. I took on summer jobs working in direct care and seasonally during breaks at this particular facility and had come to love what I was doing. I was working in a supervisory position, writing individual care plans for residents and training staff on the proper implementation of each. I was 22 years old. I enjoyed this job and was quite successful in this position for just about 8 years, but shortly after that, something was missing. I needed more. I had yet to realize my purpose in this world.

It was during this time I decided to go further and pursue higher education. I pursued a master's degree in Counseling and Human Services while continuing to work at the facility. During this time, I also interned with the Department of Youth Services, counseling adolescents adjudicated of domestic violence. This proved to be an incredible challenge for me as I quickly broke the first rule of counseling; do not get attached. How in the world does one avoid getting attached to children in need? I continued to try. Upon completion of my degree, I left my position at the facility to pursue other opportunities in Counseling. I became a case manager for Children and Family Services (CFS) of Cleveland. I knew the moment after having to remove an infant child from her mother that this job was more than I could handle. I left CFS after just six months in the position. It was simply too much for me to bear.

After my short stint with CFS, I was invited to come back to the facility where I had previously worked and was promoted to a Director's position. Maybe this was purpose? I was efficient in my work, I was able to make great connections with residents, their families, and the staff, and I was an effective leader in the organization. I had watched my father lead a large organization and learned about effective leadership while growing up. When he spoke, his staff always listened. Not because he was the boss necessarily, but more so because he took an interest in what they had to offer and demonstrated such passion in his vision for the local community. I wanted to impact the world in a similar fashion. Although I enjoyed the work I was doing as a Director, I was still unsettled. Reflecting on my many experiences, I determined that the one area of consistency, no matter which capacity I worked, was teaching. I made the decision to pursue a career in teaching and back to school I went. Unfortunately, this did not sit well with the CEO of the residential facility and I was forced to resign to fulfill my student teaching responsibilities. It was an unfortunate, but vital event that taught me growth, tenacity, and perseverance. I completed my course work and received my first teaching position in 2000.

While working to find and define my passion over all of those years, I went through several other transitional periods. I got married and taught for some years in the largest district in our area, and yet, I continued to struggle determining my passion and purpose in this life. After the birth of our daughter in 2006 and taking some time to reflect on next steps for my life while on maternity leave, I decided to go on to pursue yet another degree. This time, I chose to pursue a doctorate degree in Teacher Leadership, which I successfully completed in 2013.

In my 20 plus years of employment, I've been through so much and gone through many changes. I proudly reflect on the fact that I continued to flourish academically throughout my academic career simply because of that one semester in undergraduate school when I realized I could. My success didn't come until I believed in myself. While I did not fulfill my dream of becoming a child psychologist, I have found that my search for GREATNESS will better serve students, teachers, and other leaders in the classroom and various workplaces. That is my passion and my purpose.

This book is designed to help you, the reader, reflect on your life and ultimately, your practice. It highlights many of my experiences, many of which you may have experienced yourself. It is a compilation of experiences, lessons learned, and changes that professionals experience in their workplace, be it a school building, business office, or other organizations. It is written to challenge your thinking and encourage a stronger mindset, promote a more positive attitude toward your craft or practice, and build effective leadership skills. While the views in this book are my own, I hope that they will allow others to find their passion and purpose in life through the process of defining their own G.R.E.A.T.N.E.S.S.

Chapter 1: Rebuilt, Not Broken

Teaching was NOT my initial career path. In fact, initially, I had wanted to be a therapist and I knew I wanted to work with children for certain. I finished my bachelor's degree and then my Master's in the areas of psychology and counseling respectively. By the time I had finished my internship working with adjudicated youth domestic violence offenders, I knew that this field was not for me after all. I began to rethink this teaching thing. I wanted to touch the lives of children in an auspicious way. Maybe teaching was the field for me after all. So, I took the courses I needed, and I began my teaching career in January 2000.

My first position was in a catholic school teaching middle school level English Language Arts. I had a great mentor that guided me every step of the way. It was a great experience, but it wasn't quite what I was looking for. I knew this wasn't my niche. I wasn't comfortable here. I didn't have a feeling of accomplishment. In fact, it was through this experience that I realized that middle school grades and I were NOT a good match at all. I ended up leaving at the end of the year for a full-time position in one of the largest districts in the state of Ohio.

I started in a third-grade classroom. I can remember being excited about having my own classroom, but also being timid and unsure. I recall thinking to myself, "Now that I have my own classroom, what do I do?" Everything I had learned in my education courses had begun to run together. What's the "curriculum"? What about lesson plan writing? And, wait! What about behavior management plans? Oh, my goodness! What in the world had I gotten myself into? There was so much I still needed to learn and yet, I was about to be responsible for a classroom full of children.

Thankfully, the principal under whom I was hired was incredibly supportive and encouraging. She gave me sound advice about how to get started and paired me with a veteran teacher who was very knowledgeable, down to earth, and didn't present herself as intimidating in any way. Suddenly, my anxiety lessened. This veteran teacher mentored me the entire year. She was always willing to help me work out my lessons and to make them more fun and exciting. I felt comfortable that this was it. This was where I was supposed to be! That is, until my principal was replaced halfway through the year. What little comfort I had, had now been taken away. To this day, I am still unsure of the reason(s) behind her replacement. What I knew, for certain, was that things would be changing for me and soon. Little did I know how drastically.

Thankfully, I did survive my first year and was preparing to enter my second. This particular school year (2001-2002), I was placed in a fourth-grade classroom. I had a new team, a new curriculum, and now, a new principal to learn as well. She was a strong woman and had entered the year with the clear intent to shake things up and turn the school around. She communicated to the students that there would be no "ruckus" tolerated by any means. She instituted the "zero tolerance" plan from day one. She was straightforward with parents, although her approach frequently lacked tact and was very rough around the edges. My new team consisted of two knowledgeable and very creative teachers. In fact, I remember sharing with them, wishing I had inherited a creative, artistic gene, but, my plain Jane ways would have to suffice for the moment. They appeared to be willing to help me learn the new curriculum and helped me obtain materials that I would need to complete my lessons effectively. I was beginning to feel things might work out after all. That's what I thought. Unfortunately, things became very bad for me very quickly.

I must admit that I have suppressed many of my memories of this time because those years ultimately became my hell on earth, but I will share as accurately as my memory allows. My first hint that these years would become a tormenting thorn in my side was during one of our first staff meetings. I remember the principal coming in and announcing that our school was in a state of academic emergency. Our scores were among the lowest and our students were not making sufficient gains. Rather than devising a recovery and remediation plan, she instead stated something to the effect that, "…whatever happens, I am NOT going down with this ship! That you can be certain of!" I was in utter disbelief! Did she really just say that? I thought perhaps my hearing might be failing me. She couldn't have made that statement. I could have settled for my failed hearing at that moment, only she repeatedly made it a point to announce this chilling declaration, both frequently and emphatically!

Over the next two years, she continuously challenged everything I did and every move I made. Even worse, the anxieties and insecurities regarding my knowledge base, instructional practices, and delivery, which I thought I was sharing in confidence among my team, I later found was being shared with my principal, after practically all of our "team" meetings together. I knew confidentiality had been broken because my principal would reiterate certain ambivalences I shared with my team in [private] conversations, sarcastically and humiliatingly, directly and indirectly. She would intentionally exclude me from professional development in-services meant for the entire fourth and fifth grade teams. Even more than that, she would engage my co-workers in slanderous conversation about how ineffective I was as a teacher with the intention of these conversations getting back to me upon their return. She would look at me with a condescending smirk that would pierce me to my core.

I couldn't understand what I had done to deserve this treatment. I just wanted to learn what good teaching was all about. I wanted to be the best teacher I could be. That's all! There are so many other things I could relay about those years, but that would ultimately give power to those negative connotations, and that would be absolutely counterproductive to my purpose with this book. I will share, however, this one last memory with you because it does lend itself to my professional growth and development. During what was probably my last evaluation with her, I shared my aspirations of one day becoming an administrator and wanting opportunities to learn as much as I could in order to reach that goal. Her response was very cold but not at all surprising. "You barely make an effective teacher, let alone making a good administrator." She added that the only reason she challenged me and pushed me so hard was because she was trying to encourage me to become a "shining star". She was trying to help me. She said this to me all the time. I found it interesting, however, that she was never able share with me any suggestions for how to become this bright star she desired me to be. The only thing she offered was that it was my job to "figure out how to do that". For over two years, this is what educational leadership looked like to me and I knew in my heart that I was being failed as a developing educator. There was nothing I could do about it at that time.

For the next two years, I went to work with a headache, left work with a headache, and worked at home hour after hour with a headache, trying to "figure it out"; how to shine with no intelligible feedback received from anyone. I was in a downward spiral, moving quickly, until the best thing that could happen to me, did happen to me. I received my pink slip in November 2002! Never in a million years would I find relief in receiving a pink slip! At the end of the year I would be laid off and had decided I was done with this. DONE! I was leaving education! My principal, this "educational leader" (for lack of a better description), had literally abused me mentally, verbally, and emotionally to my breaking point. My hopes and dreams had successfully been crushed; broken into a million pieces. The insecurities and lack of confidence I began teaching with were now multiplied ten times over. Maybe she was right. Maybe teaching wasn't my thing after all.

Thank goodness for family! My mother, a retired teacher, my father, a force in the nonprofit business world, my brothers and my wonderful husband ALL discouraged me from leaving teaching. They knew more than anyone how much I adored children, how much I could enjoy teaching, and how much GREATNESS I had within. I, on the other hand, wasn't quite sure they knew exactly what they were talking about. Clearly, they hadn't paid attention to the lack of growth I had made in my current assignment. Nonetheless, with great reservation, I adhered to their counsel. Soon thereafter, I attended a minority job fair. Interestingly enough, the longest line in the place was for job openings in the district where I had just been laid off. Imagine that! Well, I certainly did NOT intend to go back there, so...I went to the shortest line in the place, to a smaller urban district, where I ultimately taught for the duration of my career, 15 years to be exact. That's right! I stuck with teaching.

I was hired as a fourth-grade teacher; the second fourth-grade teacher in the school. My mentor teacher was AWESOME! We are close friends even to this day. She helped me more than I had ever been helped in the past. Not only did she help me learn the curriculum and the procedural processes of the school and district, she also taught me time management and stress management. Someone cared about my well-being? What the heck??? I wasn't used to this at all. And my principal, this time a man, checked in on me often, as did the superintendent. They checked in very often and knew me by my name! My principal reminded me a lot of my dad. He encouraged me to interact and ask my coworkers questions regarding instructional practices and procedures before coming to him. I could respect that. He wanted us to be responsible and accountable for our own growth. Very similar to the expectations we hold to our students. The difference here was that if I did have a question or concern no one else could answer, he could and would provide instructional direction so that I would grow professionally. He challenged me to be better and gave me the guidance I needed to truly define myself as an effective educator. Year after year, I experienced the same thing. Every administrator and most every teacher I interacted with was willing to help me and wanted to see me grow, succeed, and acquire my goal. Rest assured, however, due to my earlier experiences in teaching, being a principal was NOT that goal and I'm absolutely okay with that. Because I was denied so many opportunities for growth and development, I had come to realize that my purpose was broader than the Principal's office.

This new district helped me rebuild myself into a confident and secure teacher and now, a teacher leader. I started by simply regaining my confidence in the classroom. Then, I began slowly allowing myself to experience leadership roles on small committees and also decided to pursue my doctoral degree at the same time in, of all things, Teacher Leadership. This teaching thing had me feeling pretty darn good at this point. I was feeling reassured, but I needed more. I received a new position as a School Improvement Coach, which gave me a great deal of leadership responsibilities. I really enjoyed that position because it was during my time in this position that I realized, without any uncertainty, that being a school principal was not for me. I wanted to work with teachers. I wanted to teach teachers about best practices in education and school improvement. I wanted to motivate and support teachers in their growth. I wanted to provide teachers with everything I didn't receive in those first three years of my teaching career. Eliminated after only two and a half years, the loss of that position has not deterred me from continuing to pursue leadership roles for my school and district, as well as starting my own business as an Educational Consultant. Those earlier years really took a toll on me, but, today, I am no longer broken. I have been rebuilt and I am much stronger because of those experiences.

I assert to you that true educators absolutely know that teaching is their passion. I also submit that there are those few that are in the field for three paid breaks a year, to include summers off. You know that's true and you're probably thinking about that particular colleague right now. There are also those that will make it their business to break you down. Know that this has nothing to do with you. It is done because your passion for what you do has stirred up their own insecurity, much like that of my inadequate and ineffective "principal". I've always known that teaching is where I was supposed to be. If you know, without a doubt that you are working within the realms of your passion, don't ever allow anyone, not a teacher or administrator, berate you, your practice, or your intentions. There will be times when something occurs during your day to day routine that will make you feel as if you have reached your breaking point. Trust me when I tell you that those moments are simply called challenges and opportunities for growth. They are set before you to make you a stronger problem solver, a stronger leader, a stronger individual.

Something occurred to me during one of my post-evaluation conferences which triggered these memories from my first three years of teaching. It was nothing my principal had done or said during the conference. In fact, everything she saw and rated, I agreed with. While it was difficult to pinpoint, I believed it may have been triggered by my lack of knowledge in a newer instructional process. I felt this overwhelming feeling of failure as a teacher leader and it broke me down into that insecure, timid first year teacher I thought I had left behind. The time had come for me to define my own greatness. I knew that I was an excellent educator, so why was it that I had allowed these memories to torment me so? That time had long gone and passed. It was time for me to redefine myself as a leader; not only for myself, but for aspiring leaders following behind me.

I assure you; it IS possible to rebuild a broken, beaten down spirit. This by no means, suggests that we will not become unsure, unstable, and fall at times. That is the nature of life, the nature of being. It is the nature of our ever-changing field. We just will. We are always changing, learning, and growing. What it does mean, and what I have learned through my traumatizing experiences, is that we are resilient. We have the great ability to bounce back and become stronger than ever when provided with adequate support and resources. Realize that the implications of that may have altering effects on your students' thinking and willingness to become successful individuals as well. We tell them never to give up, to keep trying, and to redefine their future. Let us lead by example, knowing that when we have been broken into millions of pieces, we can pick up those pieces. Protect them from being crushed or tampered with any further. Reorganize them in order to create a stronger foundation. Be confident about what you know and what you continue to learn. You are here for a reason. Education is not for everyone. Reevaluate the way you think about teaching and learning.

Changing your thinking can affect your students' thinking as well. Remember, there is power in positive thinking! After you've done all of that, then, rebuild yourself into a stronger, more defined and effective educator and leader! Follow my journey as I share with you the ways in which I defined my greatness as an educational leader. It's been a long, hard road, but, I promise you, if education is your passion and children are your purpose for being here, redefining yourself will be a much welcomed challenge! In the following chapters I will share my GREATNESS model for leadership development, written at a time when I needed to recognize the characteristics that helped me redefine myself and become a more effective leader and agent for change in the classroom and beyond. It will provide structure and purpose to your practice, whether in education or another profession.

Chapter 2: Growth Mindset

I can remember while growing up, my parents (in particular, my dad), would tell my brothers and me that we could do and be anything we wanted if we simply put forth the effort. Good wasn't good enough. We were expected to be the best! Well, the "best" relatively speaking that is. Regardless, we all knew that our parents expected great things from us, and nothing less. We just needed to get our minds right, meaning, we needed to shift our mindset.

You're probably thinking that this might be a great deal of pressure for our adolescent minds, and you would be correct in that thinking. I can remember being so proud of bringing home a 'B' in a class, just to hear, "That's good, but why not an 'A'?" My feelings were immediately crushed! I could **not** for the life of me figure out what in the world my parents wanted from me. After all, I was doing *my* BEST!

Dad lectured us all the time about settling for average effort. I would often debate him saying that a 'C' was passing and passing is a good thing! That's what my teachers told me. He always countered with the explanation that while it **is** true that a 'C' is passing, it's passing with "average" effort. He would emphatically add, "YOU are not average. You are better than that. You *can* be and *are* ABOVE average!" My academic records would suggest otherwise, however. I was in average classes and the few advanced placement courses I tried, I struggled in and ultimately dropped, so, for me, and there was no evidence of being above average in my immediate view. In retrospect, I needed to truly define the word "average". It is what I believed myself to be and I needed to understand why. A self-fulfilled prophecy I had created for myself, a fixed mindset; a belief system that ultimately stunted my academic growth and development since "average" is all I believed I was capable of being.

Dad did all he could do to encourage me to snap out of this mindset throughout my high school career. He even began to bribe me with money and gifts for every "good" grade I would bring home while my focus turned more and more towards sports than academics. Don't get me wrong, I put in just enough effort to graduate and go on to play volleyball in college! Sports had become my primary focus. I excelled in athletics and continued to be average in academics. I STILL made it to college, played volleyball, and went to my average classes while continuing to excel athletically. In my eyes, I'd made it. I was successful!

While in college, I knew I still had a job to do. My parents paid a lot of money for me to go away to college and I knew I had to perform academically. I was prepared to do my "best" and obtain those same average grades in college, just as I had done in high school. Oh, I followed the subliminal messages my parents sent me while I was away. I went to classes on time and attended every day. Listen... I'm not ashamed to say, I was afraid to miss a class! I'm telling you, my parents could see me 500 miles away skipping classes!! So, I did what I was expected to do to receive those same average results I was used to. Only, for the first time, I received straight A's! This was unexpected and unintelligible to me. I was stunned and excited to finally be able to experience what it meant to be ABOVE average.

Those straight A's would significantly change my mindset moving forward. All those years my parents spent telling me I could, I negated and told *myself* I couldn't because I was convinced I was nothing more than average. I believed that for many years leading up to that point. I had finally seen for myself what real time and effort could accomplish. Something incredible happened that first year in college. My expectations for myself changed. There was a distinct shift in my academic behavior and expectations. I'd come to the realization that what I originally considered to be effort was my acceptance and belief that the limitations implicitly placed on me by my teachers and subsequently, myself were true. Not all of my teachers, but enough of them to influence my self-perception to become my own reality. They instilled in me the perception that I was average and I simply settled for that. What I thought was pressure from my parents I came to understand was a manifestation of their own experiences and a buffer to shield us from the indiscretions of the world they had seen growing up.

Experiences from the Civil Rights Era of degradation and depreciation shed light on what I thought were pressure. It wasn't pressure at all! It was simply their way of communicating to me that I should never allow anyone, or any circumstance dissuade me from accomplishing my goals. What they tried to instill in me was a growth mindset. A belief that the world was mine for the taking! All I needed to do was believe that. It took me years to understand that notion. Later, as a teacher leader of elementary school students and fellow educators, I shared the same passionate message I'd received growing up.

With this new awareness, I had come to realize that you never really know what students are dealing with when they walk into your school building. Like me, they all have a unique story that contributes to their efficacy and mindset. You may have some indication or inkling of students' lives based on the demographics of their surroundings, but unless it is communicated, you are driven by assumptions. You'd be surprised at some of the stories I've heard from students. The reality of their unfortunate circumstances was often followed by statements such as, "I couldn't finish my work" or even more irresolute, "I want to go to college, but I'm not smart enough!" I found this so disheartening, but rather than feeling bad, I used this to fuel my passion to help them build the mental capacity to change their circumstances.

This led me to ask myself the following question, "What do you expect, Kelly?" What do you expect from your students? Do you expect them to achieve at the bar that we lower so often for students to see and feel success? Or, do you expect to raise the bar so exceedingly high that it is out of our students' reach? I worked to find a happy medium. Some researchers suggest meeting students where they are. I agree only to an extent. I understand that developmentally, students need to experience success at their academic level, but at what point do you stop focusing on what we cannot change as teachers and begin empowering students to reach higher than normally expected in order to change their circumstances for themselves? As educators, you cannot change societal circumstances, but you can control the level of expectations placed on your students.

I'm not suggesting that I have the answer, but I intrinsically believe that a teacher's expectations can present long-lasting effects on students. I understand that societal limitations can be a great barrier for students, but until they develop a new mindset, an undisclosed mindset, cultivated from deep within them, they will continue to resign to the confines of their circumstances. To combat this, I spent some time thinking of ways to shift the mindset of students in the same way my father did for me.

It was 3:20 pm on the Friday before winter break during the 2013-14 school year. I drove home in complete silence that day, reflecting on the events of the day. Every part of my soul wanted to be thinking about the holiday parties I would be attending, the fellowship with family members I would enjoy, and of course, the rest I had so eagerly longed for during the last few weeks. Stress had begun to build and everyone, students and teachers, were ready to go! However, this was not at all what consumed my thoughts. A student touched my inner core this week. I will come back to this shortly.

As I drove home that day, encased within my silence, I began thinking of the "Scholar Statement" I'd written just the summer before. It read as follows:

> *I am a Scholar.*
> *I can DO anything, LEARN*
> *anything, BE anything.*
> *I cannot fail and WILL NOT fail,*
> *Because failure is not an option.*
> *I am in control of my future and*
> *my destiny.*
> *I am a Scholar.*
> *I am the FUTURE.*

I'd written this after spending some time thinking of ways to help my students' change the way they think about learning. I had recently visited a local charter school and done some research on the Uncommon Schools; drawn to the approach used to help students focus on a future filled with success. I found that inside the walls of these schools, student classrooms are typically named for colleges and students were referred to as scholars, thus committing to reinvent students' thinking from that of a fixed mindset to a growth mindset. In a 2012 interview, Carol Dweck clarified the difference between the two mindsets as follows:

In a fixed mindset, students believe that their basic abilities, their intelligence, their talents, are just fixed traits. They have a certain amount and that's that, and then their goal becomes to look smart all the time and never look dumb. In a growth mindset, students understand that their talents and abilities can be developed through effort, good teaching, and persistence. They don't necessarily think everyone's the same or anyone can be Einstein, but they believe everyone can get smarter if they work at it (retrieved December 24, 2013, from onedublin.org).

    I loved the approach and made the decision to adopt this in some form within my own classroom. The Scholar Statement had become our daily affirmation, our mantra. I needed to empower them. I needed them to embrace the greatness that many of them had yet to realize was within them. I needed them to hear it, know it, and embrace it. They are all "scholars" and were referred to as such, no matter where we were or what we were doing in the school. The Scholar Statement was a daily reminder of my expectations for them and the expectations for themselves and each other. It was a daily reminder that although they may not catch on right away or get all the questions right, they were to never give up trying. That just wasn't an option in my classroom. That's how I would push them toward their highest potential, but they had to believe it first. Ultimately, my scholars began to support and encourage each other when things became a challenge. They cheered each other on and when that one scholar wanted to give, another would say, "Keep trying! Failure is not an option!!" There was a clear shift in my classroom, and everyone could see it in motion. Soon after, many of my colleagues asked for a copy of our Scholar Statement and began using it as their classroom mantra. I began to hear more and more children referred to as scholars. This was a proud moment in my career.

    Now, back to this interaction I had with one particular scholar during our last week of 2013 together. I will call this young man Victor. On the Thursday before winter break, the school would typically attend the annual winter program dress rehearsal. This particular year, the K-2 scholars, with the exception of about 17 of my volunteer scholars, performed the program. The music teacher asked for this select group to assist the kindergarteners with one song during the program, as well as greet parents and act as runners for other classes in between songs. Of course, like a proud mother, I agreed to allow these 5th-grade scholars to participate. Victor was among the chosen.

Now, remember, knowing a scholar's story will better help you understand their thinking and their actions. Here is a bit of Victor's back story. Victor was one of six siblings. He was the third oldest. He was known to cause "problems" and instigate drama, as were a few of his siblings. However, he was also very bright, athletic, and funny. You see, I found in his academic records that Victor had the documented potential of performing at the **advanced** level on the state's standardized assessment. His scores had been on the decline since 3rd grade. His strength was in the area of mathematics, particularly with problem-solving. He especially enjoyed the challenge of solving 6th-grade problems at the time. Reading was not his best friend, but he trudged through it, generally just to pacify me. However, I knew this could all change depending on how Victor's morning began. There were times when Victor *refused* to work and instead **pouted** in protest against daily assignments. His inability to process frustration at any given moment would block his ability to complete daily work tasks. There were times when he was confronted with something that would push him to the point of giving up. He did not and would not believe that there was more to his mindset. Like mine at that age, it was fixed! So, rather than exerting more effort, he chose to revert to behavioral disruptions instead.

On that day, that Thursday before break, I remember Victor was in rare form. He was all over the place, excited, off task, and in anybody's ear about anything insignificant (albeit significant enough to get under everyone's skin)! He had become quite skilled at doing things under my radar. Normally, I was able to detect even the slightest thought of becoming disruptive, but on this day with so much going on, I admit he was two steps ahead of me.

As we waited for the other grade levels to arrive for the performance, I noticed one of my girls crying uncontrollably. I had been sitting in view of them and hadn't noticed anything out of the ordinary, so I was caught off guard at the sight. I knelt and asked her what was wrong. She proceeded to tell me through each crying breath that Victor had been calling her names and how extremely tired she was of him teasing her. Victor avoided eye contact with me at all costs as I spoke with her, so I already knew something was up. He was even talking to himself under his breath and I knew he was trying to convince himself that he did not care that she was telling me what he had done. My stare had become a glare and Victor's eyes had finally met mine. I motioned for him to take a seat on the bleachers and allowed the young lady to go to the restroom to get herself together.

I was SO upset with Victor and I began to scold him. "Scholars are respectful to each other and other people!" I scolded. Then, I stopped. I had to approach this differently. He had been yelled at and scolded enough. Probably more than imaginable but that was an uncertainty and was also irrelevant at that particular moment. What was important right at that moment was how I *chose* to address Victor about what had happened between him and this classmate on *this* particular day. I waited a few moments before speaking with him. We both needed a moment.

Moments had passed and I was ready to talk, so I called Victor over to me and away from his peers. I asked him what happened. He admitted to calling her names, but only *after* she called him names first. Now, this next statement will seem a bit cliché, but I have to say it…she was the student that *never* said a word and was *never* in trouble, so needless to say, it was difficult for me to believe this accusation; I continued to listen anyway. I shared my reservation with Victor, and he understood my dilemma. I thanked him for his honesty and understanding at that moment. It was at this point that I shifted the conversation from his admitted negative behavior to his positive and greater potential.

I told Victor that he was filled with greatness. I told him how smart he was, in addition to being athletic and humorous. I told him that he could do anything he wanted to do in the world, but that he had a bad habit of blocking his greatness from shining through with the continuous choices he was making inside and out of school. I explained that hurting people was simply a way of blocking the good that was inside of him. I told him that it was okay to be smart and to show other people that you *are* smart. I told him that he was (and was allowed) to be a great example for his peers. I encouraged him not to be ashamed of his ability and to use his greatness to change his circumstances and the world around him. Victor said nothing. Tears began to stream down his face instead. I asked him why he had begun to cry. He again said nothing. I asked if he had ever been told that he was smart and filled with greatness. As he wiped his tears, he still said nothing. He only shook his head indicating he had not. My heart sank at that very moment. I thought about Victor and that conversation for the rest of that evening.

On the last day before break, Victor was…different. It's on this day that we *all* expect shenanigans and overzealousness from our scholars, so I expected Victor to respond in-kind. This time, however, I was wrong. Victor came in reserved and stoic. Rather than sitting with the other young men that had congregated to work on the holiday packet, Victor sat alone. Don't get me wrong, he did not withdraw himself entirely. I could tell that he was making good choices, purposefully and consciously, throughout the day. It took my reflecting on the events of the day to realize what had happened. Victor had heard what I said and had begun thinking about his potential. He even hugged me and wished me a Merry Christmas before he left. The best gift I could have ever received that year. I have to admit; I cannot help but wonder if this change in mindset continued after he left me.

My reflection revealed that your approach, as educators, truly matters. What you say and how you say it, what you do and how you do it, matters! Your actions and words can have transformational effects on your scholars' mindsets and lives. One word, one phrase, one spoken sentence is all it takes to make or break a scholar's spirit. One word, one phrase, one spoken sentence can change their mindset in the blink of an eye. That's quite a bit of power and responsibility to have as educators. However, I also realized that this duty comes with the territory. Teachers have committed to taking the good with the bad. It is my opinion that educators have changed the meaning of that statement. You see, what often happens is, those terms, "good" and "bad" are taken and used to *label* the scholars that you serve. Stop and be honest with yourself. You've done it! We've all done it. "He's good." and "She's bad." But, let's be quite clear, we should not consider "good" and "bad" to be definitions of our scholars' behaviors but rather an indication of an inability to communicate their needs and/or the lack of guidance they may or may not receive outside of school.

> *"What you say and how you say it, what you do and how you do it, matters! Your actions and words can have transformational effects on your scholars' mindsets and lives."*

I'm not sure what direction my life would have taken had it not been for that first semester in college. Had I not realized the greatness I had to offer, I may have remained fixed in my mindset for many years beyond college. I know now that it is because of that semester in college that I am the educator I am today. It was a defining moment in my life.

I share this story every year with scholars just like Victor and me. I emphasize, "You're **not** average and your circumstances **do not** have to define you. If you expect great things, you will do great things!" What happens is beautiful. The more scholars hear how great they are, the more they come to believe it! The shift of a child's mindset is one of the most gratifying transformations a teacher can witness.

Reflection:

How do you model a growth mindset? How will this help you connect with your scholars and colleagues?

_____

_____

_____

_____

_____

_____

_____

_____

_____

_____

_____

_____

Chapter 3: Reinvent Yourself

It only takes a few months to get to know your scholars. In that time, you come to recognize when they are sick, when they are happy or sad, when they have mastered a skill, and certainly when they are struggling. You especially come to recognize very well their strengths as well as their weaknesses. It is also during this time that you should notice your own instructional habits and practices. You may, at times, find yourself comparing the predicted success of this year's class with that of last year's class. Perhaps that's just how I entered each year, but the fact of the matter is, that thinking pattern never seemed to fail. I always found myself comparing my current practices and outcomes with past practices and outcomes. This type of reflection is not a bad thing, assuming you are doing something with what you find.

You may be looking at this in disagreement, thinking this isn't you at all. You might be thinking that there is no need to compare because you are doing what you have always done and, well, quite honestly **that** is precisely my point. I know you have heard the saying, "you need to work *smarter,* not *harder"* at some point during your training or career. Remember the half-day teacher in-services you attended to help you put together your instructional strategy "toolbox"? Or the professional development that suggested that you refrain from "reinventing the wheel" because "if it ain't broke, don't fix it?" I have heard all of these more often than I'd like to admit! I have always interpreted these phrases to mean, do nothing more and do nothing less than what you have always done. Use what you already have and don't tarry too long on any one skill.

I could not see how any educator could make sense of this contentious thinking; this ridiculous thinking that educators need not change with the current times. I admit, early in my career, I adopted this same thinking. I had become comfortable with such phrases because that's what the educators around me had taught me and done. But, after some years in the classroom and having given this some deep thought, I had become disappointed with myself and convicted for falling into such disregard for not only my teaching, but more importantly, my scholars' learning. I would like to think that it was the vast practical, constructivist approaches and experiences I had acquired along my journey that ultimately opened my eyes and helped me to realize just how truly foolish I was to believe that there was no need to put more effort into my practice. I found that there was no growth, personal or professional, in this complacent way of thinking. With any gift or skill, as you well know you must continue learning, practicing, and developing in order to perform at your best. Although I knew this to be true from experience, I still had the audacity to think this did not apply to me in the classroom.

Think about this. Every year, classroom teachers receive new scholars. They are different in appearance, different in the way they behave, different in the way they learn and process. Yet, each year I've witnessed educators reach into their bag of "tricks" and teach scholars, knowingly, with all their differences, the *same way* they have always done, continuously expecting different learning outcomes and results. You might recognize this as the definition of insanity as defined by Albert Einstein and appropriately enough, this is exactly the mind frame I watched educators succumb to. This bears the following question; if your scholars are continuously changing and evolving, why shouldn't your instructional practices change and evolve right along with them? In my opinion, it only makes sense to reinvent our instruction to meet the needs of our scholars; however, I think many educators have thought it unnecessary simply because using what they already have and what they already know makes what they do *easier*. Contrary to popular belief, teaching is far from easy.

Let me take a moment to shed a little light on what I am saying here. Five years ago, while considering this idea of "not reinventing the wheel", two concepts came to mind that my scholars seemed to struggle with every year along with the tools I would use to address them. The first concept was that of *making inferences*. When practicing inference, I had always used a set of inference cards obtained during the first few years of my career, somewhere around 2001. The cards provided a short scenario and included a few guiding questions which allowed scholars to infer (that is to guess or draw a conclusion) what the scenario was really about. The following is an example of a sample scenario that scholars would be presented:

> *Three brothers lived in the same town not far from each other, each with their own residence. They each built their own homes, but they each had different tastes in design and only one built his home with the best of the best materials. The brothers worked hard every day to outsmart the town bully who would never leave them alone. The bully always followed them around trying to ransack their homes.*

Now, **you** may recognize this short piece as a rendition of the fairy tale, "The Three Little Pigs", but I found out quite quickly that when scholars had not been exposed to these early literature pieces (and there were many that had not), then my inference cards were no longer useful. Yet, rather than reinventing the activity with something that was real and relevant to my scholars; rather than reinventing my instructional strategy and practice to meet the needs of my scholars; I used these cards which to them, were meaningless! Yet, every year, I would repeat the same activity with the same scenarios thinking, "*This* year, they will get it!" I had finally had a much-needed epiphany. If children are unfamiliar with the literature and the cards bring confusion, why on earth did they continue to make it into my toolbox of strategies? I challenged my thinking further, wondering why I continued using this same strategy, with a different group of scholars; why did I continue using the same instructions, with the many different learning styles and experiences sitting in front of me expecting different outcomes from the lesson, when it was clear that following through with the lesson did nothing but cloud my scholars' understanding. It was, by all appearances, a never-ending and all too familiar cycle I had gotten myself into simply because it was easy and because I wasn't supposed to the work into reinventing the metaphorical wheel.

The second concept that came to mind was that of working with fractions. During this unit, I would generally have each scholar color and cut out fraction bars to use as a resource. I used the bars to teach equivalent fractions and comparing fractions. It had proven to be an excellent resource for scholars in the past, assuming they would cut them out accurately and were able to keep up with them inside their desks. It was in essence, a glorified art project, with explicit mathematical intentions. At least that's what I led myself to believe. Yet, every year, I would have those few scholars who would lose their fraction bars, cut them out inaccurately, or never came to understand that this activity was more than a coloring and cutting project. Yet again, with every year, this fraction bar activity made the toolbox of strategies to include in our fraction unit. Even though it generally caused me (and them) unnecessary stress and tended to be more of a waste of time, I continued to use this activity thinking it had to work out better the next time around. When in reality, it all became my own personal insanity!!

Here is one last example. Every year, before state testing, teachers within the testing grades would practice test-taking strategies by essentially "teaching to the test". It is what we had always done. Many of you have probably done something similar in the past. For my school, however, lack of supplemental funding to pay teachers outside of regular school hours stifled any hope of an after school program to support and strengthen these much-needed testing skills; and while some skills were embedded into daily instruction, this specific practice was completed with old assessments. Teachers practiced with their individual classes and the principal would even practice with entire grade levels. Don't get me wrong, this strategy had been quite successful in the past, however, after some changes in staffing and leadership, not so much. Even with all the effort we had put towards preparing our scholars for the state assessment, our scores would still not meet the expected adequate yearly progress and as a result, we would be ranked at the "Academic Watch" designation level for years to follow. Placed on a school improvement plan, the approach to close our achievement gap had not deviated much from what had typically been done in the past. Year after year, state assessment practice and preparation looked the same - teaching to the test. Well, it turned out that this process, for our staff, had become tedious, redundant, and incredibly stressful! We were doing the same thing, every year, changing nothing about our instruction. Had we made *some* progress? Sure we did! But, not enough progress to be recognized for making even smallest gains. Not by our state support team, not by our district, and certainly not by the board administrators.

So, how do you avoid such insanity? There must come that moment when you realize and acknowledge that something *has* to change. It is not the scholars that need to change. It is *you* that must reinvent yourself and your practice to meet their needs. It is imperative. They come to you in their best form. In order to support them and help them grow and develop, teachers need to change! When you chose education, you committed to making a conscious change; to reinventing yourselves in order to impact learning. I acknowledge that change is indeed difficult, but I submit to you that this is only the case when you are not committed to the *change* but instead committed to what's *easy*. It is time for a conscious and purposeful paradigm shift. Would you not make modifications within your life if it were necessary? Think about it. When you get tired of wearing your hair a certain way, what do you do? You change it. When you get tired of eating the same foods or at the same restaurant, what do you do? You eat something different or someplace else. What about when you get tired of watching television. What do you do? You turn it off and do something different! You see, when the change benefits *you*, you make the change. You have committed yourselves to the lives of children and the field of education. When you took those classes, completed your student teaching, and passed that test, you vowed that educating children was your passion. So, why wouldn't you change your practice to benefit them? Wouldn't you agree that they deserve that much from you? So, when your scholars change, you too ***must*** also change! Metaphorically speaking, you will not only be "reinventing the wheel" to acknowledge scholars' differences when they enter your classroom, but you essentially will be making changes in order to **refine** your wheel, making it better and more equitable for learning. That wheel you are reinventing; is *yourself*.

You have to remember that the state of education is constantly changing. This has been noted with the transition from state benchmarks and indicators to the Common Core State Standards. It has also been seen in the shift from the two-year field experience and student teaching of old to the 3-year Resident Educator and Mentoring program requirements of new. Even the teacher evaluation process has changed and continues to change. There are always changes. Difficult or not, you have chosen this field of education and committed to educating *all* children. I encourage you to get *re*committed. Take a closer look at your "toolboxes". Are the contents of your box providing rigorous learning opportunities for ALL scholars? Is it preparing your scholars to be college and career ready? Are the skills necessary for life? If the answer is no, then it is **your** job, **your** responsibility to reassess and *reinvent* what you are doing! Change your approach. Change your instruction. Get comfortable with being uncomfortable and reinvent yourself. Anything less is doing a disservice to those you serve.

Reflection:

How can reinventing yourself benefit you as a teacher? What are some things you could change right now about your practice and/or your approach?

Chapter 4: Empower

Growing up, I can remember hearing my father say, "There is ALWAYS learning to do!" For him, even when there was no homework to do, there was still something that could be learned. I remember thinking how crazy my parents were to actually encourage us to learn something new **outside** of school! I was convinced that my folks had officially gone mad! We were out of school, for goodness sake! So what *learning* was there to possibly be done? My dad would even try to persuade me to read the dictionary in my spare time, when I found myself bored with nothing to do. He was of the strong opinion that a well-versed vocabulary would be beneficial to my future. Of course, I refused to engage in such a preposterous idea, never fully understanding why he would suggest such ridiculousness. Of course, once I grew older and became an educator it all began to make sense. Once I became a parent, it became clear as day. What I had not realized in my younger years was that my parents were preparing me for what to expect once I entered college and beyond; they were teaching me to empower myself. Whether school was in or out, we were to always work to gain as much knowledge about the world as possible in order to evolve into well educated and informed leaders among our peers. This learning was not always found in books or in teacher's lessons. In fact, this learning came, more so, from the experiences and exposure to new people, places, and events my parents intentionally created for my brothers and me. All of this combined, has empowered me to become the knowledgeable leader I am today.

What exactly does it mean to be "empowered"? Merriam-Webster defines it as a verb, meaning "to promote the self-actualization or influence of". More specifically, becoming self-actualized, means, reaching one's fullest capacity through inventiveness, independence, efficacy, and a comprehension of the real world! As the saying goes, "knowledge is power". I have personally come to learn the power gained when time is taken to empower oneself with new knowledge prior to entering a new school year or other venture. This is, indeed, how educators promote and reinforce the importance of being a lifelong learner to their scholars.

Sadly, I learned pretty quickly that my scholars were not familiar with the concept of being lifelong learners. Oftentimes, they struggled to envision their lives the next week, so long-term planning was a challenge for them. For them, empowerment had confounded meaning and was not relatable to their circumstances. More realistically for them, empowerment was demonstrated by how well they could protect themselves and their siblings [with their hands]; or how loudly they could over talk their parents, peers, and teachers. Now, let me be clear. I understood how my scholars' environment and experiences affected this type of mindset; however, it also contradicted the climate I intentionally worked to instill within my classroom environment. I came to recognize that in order to empower my scholars with knowledge, they not only needed to have a concrete understanding of exactly what empowerment looked like, they needed to understand how this knowledge would benefit and impact their futures; it was my responsibility to teach them, just as my father taught me.

Without sounding too cliché, it turned out that daddy was correct after all. Not necessarily about reading a dictionary. I still don't necessarily believe I would suggest this to any scholar, although I wouldn't stop any who might be intrigued by doing it. I would want them to know, however, that the pursuit of knowledge through reading and research is equally as important as pursuing knowledge through experiences and exposures when it comes to empowering oneself. I am of the belief that the more your scholars read, the more their minds will be stimulated to draw conclusions and ideas about what is going on around them. Additionally, creating meaningful experiences and exposing your scholars to new, real world insights will allow them to make relevant connections that will promote the empowerment you are working to impress upon them. There is something to be said about a scholar that can form a well thought out explanation about something they have read or experienced. A demonstration of the ability to defend their thinking is a highly gratifying experience for any educator because this is what empowerment truly looks like.

Another important aspect of empowerment is scholars' ability to evaluate themselves as young leaders and problem solvers. This type of empowerment will bring about a growth and development that will undoubtedly reflect in the way your scholars receive and process new learning in the classroom. So many times, scholars fall into the habit of regurgitating statements that have been fed to them. Why not teach them how to analyze and productively voice their thoughts and opinions for themselves? They are already taking small chances in their tone and articulation. The problem is they tend to be inconsistent, inconsiderate, and untimely in how they express their developing empowerment. It is a display of immaturity of sorts, but, as an educator, it is your charge to help them learn how to disseminate their thoughts and feelings into well thought out, rational statements or expressions that are productive and meaningful to the particular discussion. I realize this can be a difficult and confusing task for many scholars to discern; especially those that have already been involuntarily responsible for so many grown up things in their young lives. Many of them are not used to the fact that anyone even cares how they respond to or process information. Be prepared for some resistance around this shift in paradigm, but in the end, you will see a great deal of growth and maturity in them once they begin to learn how to properly manage their newfound empowerment.

So, where exactly do you begin with your scholars? You need to be intentional about speaking *life* into your scholars' world! They need to be filled with positivity and affirmations. Encourage them to work towards pleasing themselves rather than others. Many scholars do not understand the true benefits of being empowered. Teach them how empowerment can work to benefit their own needs, both academically and personally, rather than to benefit the needs of others (that includes you!). They will need assistance identifying the moments when their empowerment has positively impacted their immediate environment, whether in conversation with a peer or teacher or as reflected in academic assignments because otherwise, they will not recognize it in its new form.

Discourage your scholars from conforming to the thoughts or ideas of others simply for acceptance. They are at an impressionable age where what others think matters. They must come to realize that the thoughts of others could, at times, potentially have a negative impact on their success. They need to understand that there will be times when taking on the thoughts of others will not mesh with what is in their minds (values and beliefs) and that it is okay. You should anticipate that this newfound independence in thinking will have the potential to become a source of frustration as scholars may continue to spend a significant amount of time trying to distinguish what their peers actually want from them. Therefore, it is equally important to teach them to take risks when dealing with their peers. Teach them to be strong and bold in their ability to say "yes" or to say "no". Scholars need to know they have a choice when it comes to making decisions that will impact their lives because if they allow others to continue to choose for them, they will be prone to being taken advantage of in the future. It can be easy for scholars to fall into the habit of saying and doing what they think others expect of them at the time, but at the same time, they need to understand that this also has the potential to diminish their power. I suspect you have probably already seen this within your classrooms.

Along my journey, I did my best to remain aware of my scholars' abilities to be easily influenced by others and need to fit in at all costs. I also understood their fear of being excluded for disagreeing with the decisions of a particular peer group. I made it my task to try to encourage them every single day to advocate for themselves in order to break this indistinguishable bind that held them from being the free-thinking individuals I hoped they would become. In fact, there were times when I would intentionally create experiences for my scholars, allowing them to have the opportunity to hear the voice that otherwise would go unheard; their own voice. It was like watching a flower bloom in slow motion. I would watch as they began to hold their heads up a little bit higher, with voices that had become a little bit louder. Pay close attention to your own scholars. You will witness them as they no longer allow themselves to be persuaded and instead, begin to trust themselves and their own voices. You will begin to notice other scholars look to them as leaders and some of their peers will begin to take the same chances themselves.

When your scholars begin to empower themselves with knowledge, you will see them experience a transformative shift in the way they approach learning. Whether through experiences or building academic skills, they will begin to think more critically and speak more confidently. Empowerment will impact how your scholars' process new ideas, thoughts, and undertakings. They will begin to speak and advocate for what they believe is right and just. Promoting empowerment affords you the full capacity to shift the mindset and climate of your scholars and your classroom, helping them to create new ways of approaching the world as they know it.

Reflection:

How can empowering yourself impact the climate of your classroom or school? How will empowering yourself benefit your scholars? You as a leader?

_____

_____

_____

_____

_____

_____

_____

_____

_____

_____

_____

_____

_____

_____

_____

Chapter 5: Accountability

Over the 18 years of my classroom and teacher leadership experience, I had not ever been told I was unsupportive and unavailable...that is until the 2014-15 school year. I am telling you, it hurt me to the core! But, being the reflective person that I am, I had to figure out how to take what I was given and respond to it in a productive manner. I had already been thinking that I'd dropped the ball; that I didn't do everything I could have or *should* have, but I found comfort in the fact that I had NEVER heard those words spoken to describe ME, not ONCE, until hearing it from this year's mentee.

I had been a leader in my school and in my district for years. I'd voluntarily served on several committees, selected as the grade level chair for my team and had also agreed to take on the role and responsibility of resident educator mentor. I admit, this may have been quite a bit to handle in a year, but I truly believed it to be manageable at the time. The fact of the matter was that I needed each and every one of those opportunities to continue to help me build my leadership skills and in doing so, I probably neglected the most important responsibility of the year, the growth and development of a young, fellow educator. It was in this capacity I had long desired to work and had been working for several years in my district, and yet, something had allowed me to suddenly fall short. I came to the abrupt realization that I may have indeed taken on too much that year; that I had finally bitten off more than I could chew. My plate was full, and my cup had runneth over! Well, I'm sure you get the point. Nonetheless, I'd been given this bit of feedback from my mentee and I needed to do something with it.

Honestly, I am not sure what I had done that led to this specific complaint. When I work with teachers, I always work to develop a non-threatening relationship and offer support in whatever areas needed. I always worked with the intention of maintaining high standards of professionalism. What I do remember is feeling some tension from my mentee and wanting to ensure this young teacher felt that I was meeting all of her needs. At this point, agonizing over the reason was worthless. I knew I needed to get to the bottom of the issue, so I confronted it. In our discussion, my mentee blamed me for her lack of learning and growing during the school year. Shocked and certainly caught off guard, I needed to respond to that. Not ever had I claimed to be perfect and I think it is safe to say that none of us are. However, I honestly believe that a sign of a great educator is the ability to acknowledge his or her actions or choices when presented with them and then holding themselves accountable for those actions or choices. When someone else points out a flaw in your leadership and/or your practice, whether education or other profession, it behooves you to correct your actions. Assess yourself. What have you done well? What needs personal and/or professional attention? Did you contribute too much? Did you contribute too little? Did you ask enough questions? Did you ask questions at all? What will you do differently next time? In answering these questions, perhaps you will find it necessary to look at your list of responsibilities and re-prioritize them. Maybe it means clearing your plate. Maybe it means searching out professional development opportunities. What I know for certain is that accountability begins with self reflection and transparency. This is not always a simple task for educators because it draws out weaknesses that many are not prepared to hear, admit, or justify.

It was not long after receiving my doctoral degree that I came to a crossroad in my life. I'd completed my degree and was not quite sure what to do with it. Sure, I had some basic ideas, but I needed to do a bit more research and reflection about my future. As I scrolled through the posts of friends, family, and associates on one social media site, I came across a post that really spoke to my spirit. A wise friend of mine wrote both encouragingly and metaphorically, of a focus on *spiritual* growth moving forward into the New Year. My interpretation of his writing suggested, learning from decisions and choices made over the last year, then releasing them while making the conscious decision not to repeat anything that ultimately had a negative impact on one's spirit or prevented one from moving forward in any aspect of their life. I found this statement to be profound and it resonated with me for several days to follow. It really helped me sort out my thoughts about the interaction I had just had with my mentee and release the disappointment I had been feeling about myself. It seemed simple enough to me and I agreed with the statement, in all its transparency, so I committed, in that moment, to do just that, reflect on what I did well and what I could do better; release all the negativity, and enter the next year with a renewed spirit.

I felt good about my decision and felt comfortable that I was on the right track; that is until another mutual friend entered our discussion with a very different viewpoint. I had grown to respect this gentleman a great deal, so when he submitted his thoughts to a conversation, my interest was always piqued. He posted to the conversation a simple question that read in part *"...reflect? For what?"* My initial thought was, well, depending on the focus of your reflection, it could potentially yield beneficial rewards. That was at least *my* purpose for reflecting. I always looked to find something good out of something bad. As we continued in our gentle opposition with one another, he made the most intriguing statement. Per usual, I was immediately drawn in. In our discussion, I described myself as a self professed "analytical reflector". He described himself as a "chalkboard", erasing things of insignificance and moving forward with that which brought him not only growth and development, but also peace and joy. Wow! A chalkboard, huh? I couldn't respond as I was caught off guard with this one. This really struck a chord. I began to think about "reflection" differently. I immediately understood this more clearly than the previous connection to spiritual growth.

You are probably wondering how this is relevant to us as educators, or even to the issue with my mentee. The relevance will reveal itself shortly, but first, I'd like to focus on this word, *reflection*. A reflection is defined in part as "a fixing of the thoughts on something or careful consideration". Now, let's add this to the idea of a chalkboard. A chalkboard is a black or green board that is written on with chalk. All you need to convey information is a piece of chalk and an eraser. If you write something on the chalkboard that is incorrect, you erase it, change it, and move forward. You may or may not recall what was once written, but there is clear evidence that something was there. Sometimes it gets dusty and messy from erasing so much, but a little residual dust does not impede the ability to move forward with conveying further information. It's quite basic and simple. In fact, I have continued to refer to this type of reflection, *chalkboard reflection*. Converse to its partial definition, a chalkboard reflection may be indicative of only *some* thoughts and/or ideas, as evidenced by the residual chalk dust (meaning, evidence that considerations existed and were taken), but the fixation on thoughts is not there. What has been said and done is just that, said and done. Erase it and move forward. There is no time for fixation, or preoccupation with matters that are out of our control. My wise friend's analogy made more sense than the previous perception I had so quickly accepted initially.

Now, let's add the idea of the more current and sophisticated Smart Board to our reflection. The Smart Board is an interactive whiteboard, which has capabilities to operate as not only a whiteboard, but also a computer and a projector, which means that files may be saved and stored for later use. Each component of the Smart Board is connected to the other wirelessly or via USB or serial cables. There are so many additional components and capabilities that I cannot begin to name them all, nor is elaboration about them necessary. What I can say with confidence, however, is that Smart Boards are indeed much more detailed and complicated than chalkboards. Now, we have what I've coined as a *Smart Board reflection*. A Smart Board reflection may be described as a fixation on thoughts and a reiteration of considerations (since several files are saved, stored, and can be referred to over and over again). While information may be erased in order to create, recreate, upload, and/or retrieve new information, those erasures can be undone, much like a word document, allowing us to go back over our decisions as many times as we feel they should be revisited and reconsidered. Well now, it appears that Smart Board reflections have the greater potential of becoming frustration, worry, and stress. Funny, I didn't feel that way when speaking about *his* chalkboard reflection.

Accountability through reflection. Chalk board reflection vs. Smart board reflection

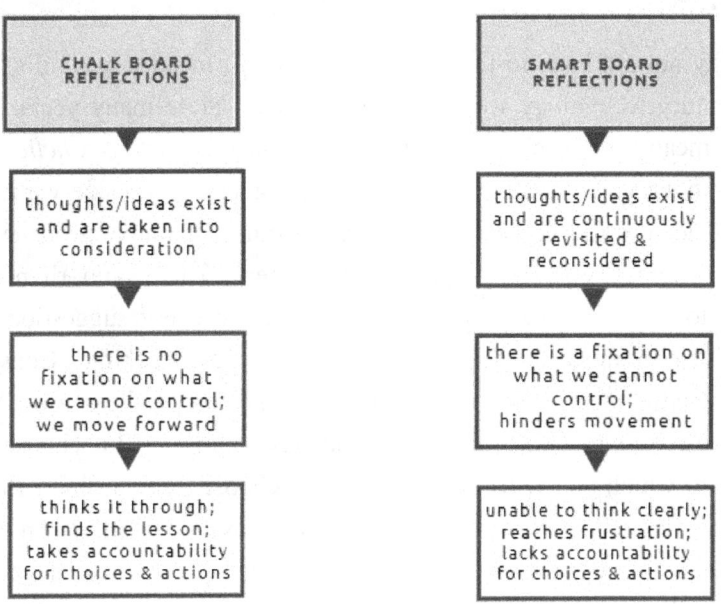

Here's the relevance. Research shows us that reflection has altering effects on instructional practice. The degree to which we reflect, and the focal point of our reflection *is* a choice we make. Why fixate on something that has happened for which the outcome cannot be changed? Why preoccupy ourselves with circumstances that are out of our control? Yes, we all would like to save the world. We all would like to protect and nurture our students. We all would like each of our students to come from the ideal home, with the ideal parental involvement, with the ideal learning environment. The same is true for teachers as learners. If teachers had it our way, we would all like teaching and learning to occur without a hitch; however, this is an unrealistic expectation of ourselves and our students. This fixation and preoccupation, this Smart Board reflection is what ultimately impedes our ability to instruct our students or provide effective leadership due to our displaced focus.

Why not get back to the basics. No, I don't mean to get rid of the 21st century technology we have longed for all these many years. Nor does it mean for a teacher leader to micromanage and act as a *helicopter* mentor over your young educators, hovering over their every move. What I do mean is, let's work to refrain from over thinking our every move. Some things that happen just happen. There's no rhyme or reason to it. It is what it is. Let's not analyze every suggestion our administrators make to mean we're not cut out for teaching. Consider this instead. If you don't over think it, it may just make sense. Yes, reflect on your practice for growth and development. But choose the *degree* to which you will reflect. Will you choose to be a Smart Board reflector, fixated on every single thought you have saved in your mental database? Think about it. You, yourself, have complicated certain considerations to the point of frustration, worry, and stress, by thinking about it, thinking about it, and thinking about it some more. I know I have. Or, will you, on the other hand, choose to be a chalkboard reflector, erasing what is irrelevant but allowing yourself to learn from the residual dust left behind? You see, you can't fixate on something that is not there. The dust, however, is evidence that there was some sort of lesson learned. Take the dust that is now on your hands and move forward into your next moment // your next lesson // your next venture.

The *degree* of reflection and the *focus* of your reflection is a choice and the choice is all yours. Be accountable for them and the decisions you make based on them, then, fix it!

Reflection:

What is the difference between Smart board reflection and chalk board reflection? Which one best describes you? How does accountability influence leadership?

_____

_____

_____

_____

_____

_____

_____

_____

_____

_____

_____

_____

_____

_____

_____

Chapter 6: Tenacity

Getting through the first few weeks of school can be incredibly unpredictable and sporadic as you have probably experienced in your career. As educators, we know all too well how quickly our rosters can change. Scholars can be withdrawn from your roster as quickly as they are enrolled. The educators work with scholars that come from a myriad of backgrounds. Some will challenge us to the point that we begin to wonder why we remain in the profession at all. I admit, this thought crossed my mind on several occasions, but it was during that 2014-15 school year that I was reminded of the reason I continue with tenacity.

I recall things were going well at the start of the year for the most part. Probably one of the best and smoothest starts to date. I had 20 wonderful scholars at the time that, in the first few weeks, brought me so much joy and reminded me of my purpose in the classroom. I began that year with 18 scholars on my roster. As I'd routinely done every year, I looked over my roster prior to the first day of school and was excited to see that I was receiving a break from some of the customary behavior challenges I'd been used to. After working with some very challenging behaviors and disabilities in the past, including a visually impaired child with a sharp tongue and a stubborn attitude, I welcomed this year's break. Some of you may even understand the exhilaration I felt! However, pretty quickly and quite expectedly, things can change at the drop of a dime when you are working in a district with a high transient population and as such; I received my nineteenth scholar just before school began on Meet the Teacher night. He was a returning student who was extremely excited to be back with us! He shared his love of school and especially reading with me on that evening! It was all too good to be true! I felt like the luckiest teacher in the school! A scholar who loved to read! I had chills listening to him share his excitement.

My twentieth scholar arrived bright and early the next Monday morning, just after I'd begun my introductory instruction. He, too, was a transfer from another school within the district. I had not received his permanent records, which was not uncommon with transfers, but in conversation, he shared with me, in a rather boisterous voice, that he was not good at math and he was very shy! His overactive, outspoken, shyness left me looking confused and had become an all too familiar sight to say the least. His first day was a prologue to the first scene if you will. As the saying goes, if it's too good to be true, it probably is. He had already made it up in his mind that he couldn't achieve and as such, would often give up and shut down. I knew this would be something I would have to work to help him through. I just needed to figure out how.

On the first day of school, I typically read a book to my scholars entitled Hooray for Diffendoofer Day, by Dr. Seuss for our first morning meeting. I used to read this book to my own children when they were younger. I found it appropriate for my fifth graders because every year, a handful of scholars would enter my class claiming they don't know anything, very similar to the experience I'd just had. The story is about creative teaching and thinking. The tale celebrates originality, differences, and uniqueness, but also ensures that each of these scholars possess the gifts and knowledge they need, not only to be successful on their high-stake assessments, but to be successful in life as well. What an amazing way to begin the school year! We acknowledged each other's differences, but I also assured all of them that they were bright, intelligent scholars that could and would be successful, but they had to trust me, trust each other, and most importantly, trust themselves.

In the days to follow, we would talk a lot about school "PRIDE" (which represents Perseverance, Respect, Integrity, Determination, and Empathy) and our Scholar Statement. We would discuss in great length each attribute of PRIDE and each line of the Scholar Statement (shared previously in Chapter 2). This was my second year using the statement and I found it to be a great guiding principle within my classroom.

I had no idea what a powerful impact it would ultimately have on my scholars. I actually recall having conversations with my colleagues about the attributes of our PRIDE guidelines and more often than not, many of us *assumed* our scholars knew them, understood them, and should be demonstrating them, especially by fifth grade. This particular year, our PRIDE guidelines were more visible in and around the school building. I had come to notice that the school wide PRIDE attributes, coupled with my statement, had begun to do something amazing to my scholars. They had begun to tenaciously demonstrate our PRIDE characteristics; encouraging each other to never give up, correcting each other's poor choices and misbehaviors, and took very seriously their role as examples for the younger grades. I was in absolute awe once I began to notice what was happening. If they were unsure of what tenacity looked like prior to this, they were beginning to understand what it meant at this point.

To put this into context, here is an example. Every afternoon, my scholars would complete a spiral math review. This review was a culmination of skills previously learned and some newly introduced skills as well. Because math had been so intimidating to most of my scholars, their initial reaction to any questioning of their knowledge resulted in a shrug of their shoulders and a typical response of, "Um, I don't know." Oh no. There it was. That fixed mindset that always had a tendency to peek its little head out right through my scholars' developing confidence. I'd thought to myself, "I just wish these children would believe in *themselves* the way that I believe in them." Before I could even offer my encouraging response, from the back of the room, like music to my ears, I heard, "Don't give up! Failure is not an option. Persevere!" I stopped in shock as I slowly looked to see who was speaking. Our Scholar Statement had been heard and understood! It felt like for the first time in 2 years, my scholars (at least one of them) got it! From that moment on, whenever anyone was stuck (including me) and felt like giving up, we all offered support to each other by saying out loud, "Failure is not an option! Keep trying!" This became an important reminder for all of us; that with tenacity, you can achieve anything.

This proved to be a profound moment in my career. There had been so many times that I would become discouraged, concerned with whether I was making a difference in the lives of my scholars. I often found myself wondering whether my expectations were too ambitious for them and whether I was doing everything I possibly could do to help them be successful. How many times a year do you find yourself doing the same thing? Educators do this all the time because we are passionate about what we do, and we believe in the capabilities of our scholars. At that very moment, that young scholar's voice in the back of the room was a reminder; a confirmation of the reason I continued to remain tenacious about teaching those young minds. I still had some lives to change. YOU have lives to change! It is the commitment you made when you entered this field. Your scholars believe in you and depend on you. No matter what the obstacle, it is vital that you continue to be tenacious about your love for teaching children. There will be challenges and they will cause you frustration, but it is vital that you remember that your scholars can succeed in spite of any obstacle or challenge.

I am reminded of a parent teacher conference that occurred that year where both the parent and I reinforced the importance of scholar tenacity. I met with a father who, first, was not required to conference for his child, and second, had not scheduled to conference for his child since he was progressing well and was demonstrating proficiency in all of his content areas. I will refer to this particular scholar as Murray. Although a conference was not necessary, Murray's father, who spoke limited English, came to see me anyway, simply to check on his son's academic and behavioral progress.

Murray was far from the typical description of a "behavior problem". He was a very talented and creative young man that had a clear understanding that his experiences inside and outside of the classroom would impact his future. He demonstrated a tenacity that was beyond his adolescent stage of development. In fact, he had become very detailed in his work and made the Merit Roll that quarter. He *did* however enjoy socializing quite a bit, which at times had become a distraction to his learning. Outside of that, however, Murray was right on track. His father expressed how proud he was of his boy, then looked at me and stated that he had always told his son that he could be *whatever* he wanted to be and that he wanted him to do better than he did himself. Of course, he did. It's what *every* parent wants for their child, right?

Murray has three other siblings, two older and one younger. They were all performing at or above grade level academically, so the father was without a doubt extremely proud, as he well should have been. Murray listened to his father proudly and intently. I looked at him and confirmed that we are *all* so very proud of his accomplishments but explained that he *still* has work to do. Even though he had worked hard to earn these grades, I explained that he must maintain his tenacity towards leading a successful academic and personal life. I asked Murray to recite a couple of lines from our Scholar Statement. I asked him, "With hard work, you can *do* what?" "Anything.", he responded. "With hard work, you can *be* what?" "Anything.", he responded. "And who is in control of your future?" I asked. He responded, "I am!" I added that it was not too early to begin thinking of his future and that he could not get comfortable with the success he had made thus far. I explained that with his tenacity, he would undoubtedly continue making the grades, but he needed to believe that he could do it and persevere through the obstacles that were certain to get in his way. His dad nodded in agreement and appreciation for the reiteration as our conference ended.

What was ironic about this entire conversation was that on the Sunday just before conferences, my pastor had given a sermon entitled "Keep it Movin". In it, he explained that attaining success in anything did not stop once you reached a set goal. You see, once you reach your goal, you keep it movin' and set a new goal! You don't stop there. You press on and you continue to fuel what is your passion *beyond* that goal. That's tenacity. How profound is that? You see, in the past, "keep it movin" meant, "go away", "get a life", "get to steppin", and "leave me alone"! But, now, in a more positive connotation, these few words could have powerful implications on you as an educator as well as your scholars. This phrase helped me to define tenacity for my scholars in a different way. In a way *they* seemed to better understand!

As educators, I recognize and understand the many challenges you face throughout a year. I know that you are charged with the task of determining the academic needs of anywhere between 20-30 scholars each year. I know that you assess each one, individually or as a group, frequently, at their individual level, many times throughout the year. I know that you assess and monitor your scholars in a variety of methods in order to predict their potential success on high stake assessments. I also know that sometimes the things you do work, and sometimes they don't. However, the fact of the matter is that regardless of the outcome, it is at that point that you make the intentional and conscious decision whether to keep it movin' or not; that is whether to demonstrate instructional tenacity or not, although, there really should be no decision to make. Nike said it best, just *do it*! When your scholars master a skill, be tenacious about your instruction by enriching and challenging them to master the next. Even when they don't master the skill, do not focus on what may appear to be your inability to reach your scholars. Keep them movin' toward building the capacity that is within them to succeed. When you become more tenacious about your instruction, you will be better able to remain focused not only on your purpose, but your scholars' learning as well. Go back to that moment when you made the commitment to serve children by becoming an educator. Check your approach, change your instruction, and be tenacious!

A scholar's inability to master a skill does not indicate an unwillingness to learn, but rather necessitates a different way of teaching in order for them to receive it, process it, and then, finally master it. It is an opportunity to define your instruction and make it better. Tenacity. When scholars master skills beyond their ability, it does not mean your job is complete. What it *does* mean, is that you have more work to do! Tenacity. It's your duty and obligation to push that scholar beyond their limits. It is your job as educators to determine just how much you can push. No matter the level of success, no matter how big or small their dream, you have to help your scholars see that even when they reach one goal, another goal is waiting in the ranks. It is important to assert to your scholars, and likewise as educators, that once you acquire one accomplishment, you must continue with tenacity to the next one! It will, none the less, be a continuum of occurring events, but I guarantee acquiring this trait will empower your scholars to become the academic leaders you are molding them to be.

Reflection:

What are you tenacious about? How can tenacity impact teaching and learning?

_____
_____
_____
_____
_____
_____
_____
_____
_____
_____
_____
_____
_____
_____
_____

Chapter 7: No Negativity

Negativity seems to have a way of seeping into several aspects of teaching and learning, no matter the grade level, school, or district. Several years ago, I was feeling unaccomplished and resentful because in my mind I had not advanced professionally as I'd initially hoped and planned. Regrettably, these feelings began to manifest and seemingly began to appear during interactions with my scholars towards the end of the school year. I found myself complaining more often, thinking to myself, "These kids!!! They just don't get it! They have no respect and they just don't *want* to learn! I don't get paid enough for this!" I would venture to say that all educators, at one time or another, have heard, spoken, or had similar thoughts. I'll be honest, after some of my worst days, I may have been liable for walking away from it all at a moment's notice. When what educators recognize as "Spring fever" sets in, scholars often become more rambunctious than ever and at the time, I was not in a good mental space to manage. For several days during this particular spring, I reflected on my practice and my approach with my scholars. My scholars' behaviors had become cold, callous, and uncaring, their level of effort lowered, and their will to learn had become almost nonexistent. I'd lost them. I spent the entire year building them up only for them to give up and throw away everything they had learned. They no longer cared. I thought negatively to myself, "Well, if they don't care, then why should I?" Then, as if right on cue and with conviction, I admonished myself. Is *this* how I **really** felt? Why had I become so negative towards my scholars and their learning? I didn't realize it then, but maybe I had contributed to their disdain in some way.

The end of the school year can be quite draining for educators. I can recall so vividly leaving my school and my scholars often exhausted, irritated, frustrated, and discouraged and these feelings had a way of hovering above me, much like a desolate cloud, as it did every year during this time. That winter had been long and cold. My scholars rarely had adequate time to release their pent-up energy since temperatures were too unbearably cold to take them outside for recess. I would like to have considered myself one who worked diligently and desperately to make learning fun but being confined to a classroom for several hours a day, every day had become so unsettling to everyone. Teachers and students alike had become restless and I, personally, was struggling. For me, there was nothing else to do except throw my hands up in accepted defeat. When I arrived home that day, I asserted to my husband, "I am DONE! They've given up and I just don't have the energy to do this another year!" He shook his head in disagreement, looked me straight in my face, and said, "Nope. That's not the type of person you are. That's not the type of teacher *you* are. So, what is **really** going on?" I looked away to hide my frustration, unable to answer.

In the same way I unconditionally love my own children, I found myself convicted once again, wretched with guilt over my current emotional struggles and uncertainties. From my very first teaching assignment to the present, I'd loved every one of the scholars that crossed my path, but there was something different about this particular group; different in ways I could explicitly identify, but also different in so many other ways I could not. Incongruity in race and ethnicity were the most obvious contrasts noticed the moment you walked into any classroom. Learning styles became apparent with daily instruction, which ultimately drew out the variations in students' self-esteem and self-worth. It is without a doubt that the unseen and unknown differentiation that make what educators do the most challenging had seemingly become the primary source of my aggravations during that time. I understood that I was only in control of that which occurred within the confines of my classroom and the school environment, but I certainly wished I could control more.

While they were in my presence, I could talk to them about hard work, challenging themselves, settling for nothing, changing their thinking, and believing in themselves; working to draw out the positive traits I knew existed within. I showed them what empathy for others looked like, good manners and respect as well. In my mind, we were a family. So, we worked to act like one by taking care of each other. We practiced building each other up with supportive words and gestures, as well as further strengthening our bond by not only learning, but by having fun in every aspect of our instructional day. I suppose this was why seeing them out of sorts, rejecting everything I had worked so hard to instill in them, hurt so very much. Referring to this as "Spring fever", as most educators do, made these behaviors look simply like child's play, however, my emotional, human side perceived it more personally as disrespectfulness and inconsideration. In actuality, it was a manifestation of the negativity that had somehow crept its way into their spirits and thus, our classroom. Their behaviors were a result of their inability to cope with their own emotions and insecurities. Because they had shown nothing but ungratefulness, I had enough and was ***done***! In my mind, I had more important things I could have been doing and focusing on rather than going the extra mile for a group of students that did not appreciate me anyway! This…I didn't need! And yet, I couldn't get any one of them out of my every thought or the depths of my beating heart. I just could not shake them.

It was time for me to face reality and the reality was this, I was in complete and total awe of the growing potential I saw in each of my scholars, not only as individuals, but also as an entire group. It was then and remains today, my belief that every child possesses a gift, that every child has the ability to learn, and that every child has greatness inside of them just waiting to come out. I was personally charged with and committed to ensuring that each of my scholars knew that before they left me each year. I wasn't certain if any of them had ever been told just how special they were before, but what I did know was that their anger and lack of self worth certainly did not come from a positive place. Therefore, I committed to making certain that my scholars reserve a space in their hearts and minds to welcome the positive feedback they were being given and needed.

I definitely had tough love for them, but I also had a gentle love that some of them, by their own admission, had only felt when I had given it to them. Reprimanding or strong correction, strong encouragement, fist pumps, pats on the shoulder, or even hugs were just some of the ways I provided positive feedback to show just how much I loved and cared for my scholars. As you are aware, state and local policies strongly discourage physical contact between teachers and students for reasons of which I was also aware and understood. However, having considered that *mine* may possibly be the *only* source of love and nurturing some of those scholars received there was no question, in my opinion, about whether to resign from the gestures. Quite frankly, the thought of ramifications never crossed my mind and never persisted very long if they did. Simply put, I just would **not** be an added source of rejection for my scholars. My scholars experienced enough negativity without experiencing it in the place they were supposed to feel safe.

When my scholars were upset, it made me upset, especially when I was unable to determine the root of their problem. When they were crying or someone hurt their feelings, I responded very much like a mother bear with every intention of protecting them from all hurt and harm, in *and* out of school. I felt very strongly that my scholars' circumstances, whatever they were, did not have to be the determining factor for the future they wished for themselves. My passion for them ran deep, so, even on days when I wanted to throw up my hands and give it all up, I knew that the inability to get them off my mind told me that I needed them as much as they needed me.

What I have experienced along my journey is that negativity breeds negativity. My negative thoughts and the negative innuendos received from others ultimately elicited ineffective instructional practices in my classroom because I allowed them to do so. Negative attitudes can set off children in the classroom and cause them to become agitated, anxious, and shut down. The circles of friends your scholars associate with, if negatively associated, will reflect in their work habits and social behavior. Therefore, you should work to instill positive social skills in all of your scholars in order to nurture healthy relationships. If the classroom is meant to be a safe learning environment, then it is your responsibility to ensure that there is no evidence of negativity within that space. In order to infuse a positive mindset in your scholars, you will need to *demonstrate* a positive mindset.

The practice of *mindfulness* is a great way to implant this into your students. Mindfulness is the practice of paying attention, on purpose, in the present, and non-judgmentally, to the unfolding of (personal) experiences moment by moment (Kabat-Zinn, 2003). That is attending to your emotions, your thoughts, your actions and learning to find the calm in all that is going on around us. Mindfulness does not require a lot of time and effort, but it does require intentionality. Consider the many instances when you find your scholars agitated and frustrated. It is during these times when you may allow what we call a *brain break*. Rather than allowing your scholars to simply take a break by talking with friends or playing a game, mindfulness practices teach scholars how to quiet their thoughts and emotions. This might be in the form of yoga or mediation, breathing exercises, or maybe even getting some fresh air. This probably sounds very familiar as it is quite possible you have practiced mindfulness before without even realizing. In a time when scholars may come in carrying with them the challenges and stresses of home and their environment, it is so important for educators to equip them with skills that will help them cope with the negativity that can sometimes be overwhelming and overpowering. Like any other skill, scholars will need to see mindfulness in action; therefore, it will be important for you to model this frequently and offer many opportunities to practice it. Embed a time during your day or a class period to practice mindfulness with your scholars. This could be at the beginning of class or perhaps before transitioning to another class. No matter how you include it, do it with purpose and meaning rather than a filler of space.

Eliminating negativity is vital to the health of your classroom community. By simply changing the way you think, the way you speak, and the way you associate with others, you will not only see a shift in the way you practice, but you will also begin to see a shift in the way your scholars respond and perform in the classroom.

Reflection:

In what ways can you work to maintain a positive attitude and mindset? What benefit will this have on your practice?

_____
_____
_____
_____
_____
_____
_____
_____
_____
_____
_____
_____
_____
_____

Chapter 8: Efficacy

Building efficacy is vital in the course of building teacher leadership and ensuring student achievement. Albert Bandura (1993) defines efficacy as "people's beliefs about their capabilities to produce designated levels of performance that exercise influence over events that affect their lives". Efficacy is about the level of confidence we as educators have in our own teaching and in guiding our students to successfully achieve in school. Even the best teachers can struggle building efficacy, however, becoming efficacious is not an unattainable goal. It can be a painful journey; one that requires reflection, transparency, and a willingness to change. Building efficacy requires educators to not only be leaders, but to challenge others to be leaders as well. My journey has been transformative as I have worked to become more efficacious every day in my practice, in how I work to develop others, and most importantly, how I lead others. Open your minds and be reflective as I help you along your journey to build efficacy and become an effective teacher leader in your building, district, and broader school community.

I'd heard it so very frequently up and down the hallways, "BE A LEADER!" As educators, we utter these words almost daily to our scholars. What exactly does it mean when we say this? Don't we have specific expectations of what it means to be a scholar leader? I would often sit and wonder how teachers could utter these words and struggle being a leader themselves. Aren't we as educators supposed to "lead by example"? That's what we tell our scholars, isn't it? Is there gratification in *not* being a teacher leader? Are the standards of expectations we have set for ourselves the reason they are so low for our scholars? It is something I have spent much of my time wondering as I am committed to my own professional growth as well as that of colleagues around me.

Think about this. What exactly qualifies a teacher as a leader? I'm going to go out on a limb here and suggest that standing at the front of the classroom is not a certifiable characteristic of leadership. There is much more to being a teacher leader than simply that. In my reflection, I began to think simplistically about the characteristics I'd expect to see in my scholar leaders in order to decipher how this might transfer to my fellow educators.

When identifying leaders in my classroom community, I would first look for those general character traits such as respect, responsibility, integrity, and accountability. I believe that these are at the very foundation of what a leader should display; therefore, it was these same characteristics that I would expect to see in a teacher leader as well. Nevertheless, for a select few of my colleagues, this was not a matter of importance or obligation. I'm not certain why this blaring lack of professional responsibility agitated me so much during my career, but, perhaps it was because I believed that as an educator, demonstrating leadership was a part of the commitment to teach. It seemed so simple and commonsensical that I assumed all educators would bring at least this much to the table.

The 2016-17 school year had been disparagingly different, even challenging for some of us, myself included. I had to stop and think on several occasions about why I continued doing this thing called teaching in the first place. At the beginning of my teaching career, I was told that I would never amount to anything as an educator, but thankfully, my scholars communicated otherwise. It was not only because of my scholars, but the many experiences I had along the way that assured me that leadership was MORE than simply respect, responsibility, integrity, accountability, and standing in front of a room with your identifiable name on the door.

The obligations of teacher leaders have the potential to bear heavy weight. As schools continue to work toward improvements, teacher leaders stand at the helm of their schools, advocating for quality and equitable education for all students. With systemic issues such as poverty, homelessness, drugs and violence at the forefront of many scholars' minds, it has become more and more difficult for teachers to encourage and motivate them to be effective learners. It becomes equally challenging for educators to be more effective and efficacious instructional leaders. Teachers are becoming more and more overwhelmed working to support scholars as they struggle to deal with the realities of their lives. As the school year passes, the days seem to get longer and harder as the end of the school year gets closer. Morale appears lower, complaints get louder, and student instruction gets done complacently enough to simply say, "I taught it". It had become clear as I walked the halls that year, that I and many of my colleagues were tired. Some were even becoming burned out. The scholars were feeling it too, expressing their frustration with outbursts and disrespectful behavior due to the lack of skills needed to express it in any other way. Relationships between teachers and scholars had begun to strain. I knew that the way in which we dealt with this sudden decline in school climate could be the difference between how successfully we led our scholars or not.

I would venture to say that being a teacher leader is indeed challenging. I would also say that it is a welcomed challenge as a teacher leader. We are in a position to be change agents in this field, but this requires commitment; commitment to change and commitment to the charge. Teacher leaders are charged with the task of identifying the issues hindering the academic growth of scholars and the instruction they are receiving. More than that, teacher leaders encourage and motivate not only scholars, but their colleagues to be the best instructional leaders they can be. Growing leaders, however, requires that teachers be open to learning new things, habits, concepts, and strategies and in that new learning, one must be willing to modify the old. There lies a thin line between one who simply teaches and one who teaches to lead. Quite honestly, it's the difference between whether you are teaching because it's your job or whether you are teaching because it's your passion.

Listen, "**BE A LEADER!**" This time, the exclamatory charge is for you, the educator. While you reflect on that, I would like to pose the following question as well. *"Why are you here?"* This might be a loaded question; however, in developing teacher leaders, it is a very important question when the lives of children are at stake. In reflecting on this question, think about not simply why you are teaching, but why are you teaching *here*, in the urban school? If you are teaching for the comfortable hours, weekends off, and the extended breaks, then teaching is probably your job, because teaching is far more than the luxury those on the outside perceive. If you have reached your wits end and find yourself in a constant battle with your scholars or have given up trying, then teaching is probably not the place for you and you should think about moving on. If you are teaching in the urban school because you believe that success is achievable regardless of background, color, disability, behavior, or other barriers, that, my fellow colleagues, is your passion. If you will go above, beyond, and to the ends of the earth to build and grow relationships, that too, is **passion**! Seriously, reflect on this question long and hard. Be honest and transparent with yourself. Why are you *really* here? The answer may be difficult to receive, but it requires your immediate response because how you answer will reveal whether you are a teacher leader, or lack thereof.

Some years ago, during a staff meeting, my principal asked us to read the following excerpt from an article entitled "What At-Risk Readers Need", by Richard Allington.

> *The bottom line is that most U.S. schools have no plan to provide the sorts of classroom instruction that at-risk kindergartners need.*

> *Neither high-quality, extensive professional development for kindergarten teachers nor expert tutorial instruction for at-risk kindergartners is on the agenda at this point. This means that most schools deliberately create a pool of students who will become struggling readers. I say deliberately because, unfortunately, that's just what it is— deliberate ignorance of what we should do to address the problems of at-risk kindergartners. (Allington, 2011)*

The above quote struck a chord with me and elicited some great discussion among a group of us during the meeting. The article discussed the lack of instruction at-risk readers receive within the classroom. Allington asserts that children leaving kindergarten not knowing their letters and letter sounds are most likely going to become struggling readers. In fact, at the time of this research, he stated that 66% of our own students were more than likely reading below grade level. Take a moment just to consider that. That means, two out of every three students in *your* classroom, are reading below grade level! Astounded by this realization, I had to stop and consider this in relation to my *own* classroom and in fact found the statement to be consistent with what I was seeing!

My thoughts clung to those two words, "deliberate ignorance". What teacher leader, in their right mind, would practice *ignorance*, **on purpose**?! Well, according to Allington, many of us tend to fall prey to this particular form of ignorance. It is a difficult pill to swallow if you really think about this and as teacher leaders, it is imperative to intentionally shift this paradigm in order for our students to achieve. Some of you may be thinking, "I would never allow this to happen!" I thought the same thing until I really evaluated my daily practice. You see, what happens is this. When we *know* that we don't know a particular instructional process or strategy to meet the needs of our struggling students, we choose to deal with our ignorance by purposely overlooking those that need the most help and focus on those we **know** we can help instead. Why? Because it's the easiest thing to do! It's just as compelling as it is true, isn't it? It was for me and, after some thought, I found, and consequently owned the fact that **I**, myself, had apparently been practicing this "deliberate ignorance" for much of that year! As a teacher leader, an efficacious leader, acknowledging this area of weakness became one of the most important moments in my career. What is done with such knowledge is what makes an educator a leader.

What exactly does this *"deliberate ignorance"* look like? I'll explain by sharing a personal experience and perception of what it looked like within my own classroom. Early on during the 2014-15 school year, I transparently acknowledged my fear of literacy instruction and development. I mean, I had enough knowledge of how to teach reading and comprehension skills to get by, but, I was a lover of mathematics and therefore, this was my area of strength. So, when it came to grammar, spelling patterns and conventions, this was a challenge for me. It had been for quite a while, and although I continued to seek help and guidance, the mere thought of being responsible for the facilitation of my students' literacy development scared me to no end. If I failed, they failed and these students are further behind than when they came to me. This was my train of thought for a very long time up to and during that year. Well, with deliberate ignorance, I had already failed my struggling readers by providing surface level intervention. I had to build efficacy in this area, but exactly how was I going to do that? I knew that ignoring the problem was much easier than addressing it, so I did what was comfortable. Because I knew I wasn't the only one facing this challenge, I was okay with publicly admitting this personal and professional flaw. In fact, for me, the public realization and disclosure signified my personal commitment to transform my deliberate ignorance into ***intentional awareness***. This was one way I could build efficacy and further develop as a teacher leader.

The following experiences are equally important when working to build highly efficacious habits (Bandura, 1997, 2008):

- **Mastery Experiences:** This occurs when one is able to set goals, work through challenges, and experience the success of reaching the goal. Once this occurs multiple times, the belief in one's ability to succeed grows, thus, encouraging and motivating us to continue persevering through future challenges and adversities.

- **Social Persuasion**: Receiving the encouragement and support of others that you have the knowledge and ability to achieve a goal.

- **Modeling Experiences:** When witnessing others demonstrate their competencies in achieving goals, one may begin to vicariously perceive themselves as equally competent.

- **Physical & Emotional Experiences:** Your physical, mental, and emotional health impact your level of effort and motivation. It's so important to take care of your health so that you can function at your greatest potential.

Additionally, it is important to highlight here that as educators who are striving to become highly efficacious, begin to look at your failures or challenges as opportunities. Work to become intrinsically motivated to set goals and commit to reaching them. For me, becoming knowledgeable and attentive to the different experiences that promote self-efficacy and choosing to become intentionally aware was a resolute, determined, uncompromising shift in paradigmatic thinking which helped me truly attend to the individual needs of my scholars. I'd become increasingly cognizant of how my scholars acquired and developed language, how they constructed the meaning of vocabulary, and how they constructed meaning from what they were reading rather than simply labeling development with a quantified number or test score.

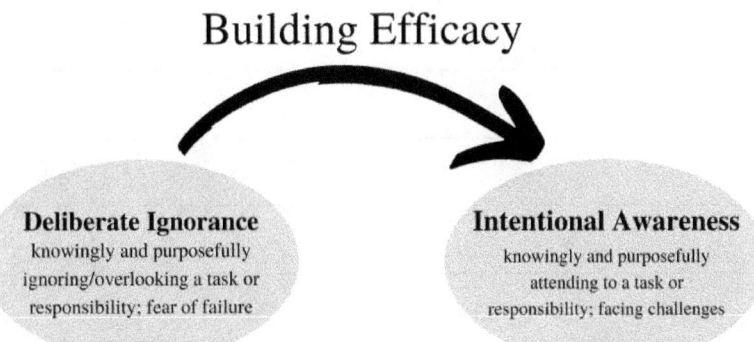

Becoming more intentionally aware and efficacious meant I was better equipped at tackling the areas of my practice that I feared so much with confidence and purpose rather than doing it only to say it was done. It meant getting beyond the surface of my scholars' learning and putting their needs ahead of my own, even when it felt uncomfortable. When I sat in reflection, I knew that becoming intentionally aware and building my efficacy would do nothing less than further align my passion with my purpose as I continued building capacity in my craft and my practice. Committing to building efficacy and being more intentionally aware requires only a simple shift in the way you think about your teaching. Rest assured that this will in turn also impact your level of effectiveness as a teacher leader.

Reflection:

What is efficacy? How does efficacy apply to leadership? In what ways can you begin to build efficacy?

Chapter 9: Stay Focused

Life has a way of leading you in different directions. Obstacles will undoubtedly get in the way of our life's hopes and dreams. What is important to remember is that obstacles do not have to mean that our goals no longer exist or that we are no longer able to reach them. Obstacles are merely opportunities for us to take a different route towards reaching our goals. They allow us to re-evaluate the steps we are taking to reach our goals. In order to reach our goals, be it personal or professional, we must remain focused on our purpose and the reason we began pursuing the goal in the first place.

For many years, I had worked at pursuing an administrative position in the school district where I was employed. Contrary to the belief of others, I had no desire to be a principal or superintendent. Instead, my desire was to work directly with teachers on the frontline to further define their instructional practices in order to directly impact their students' achievement. Unfortunately, I was overlooked on several occasions without any feedback as to why. There I was, an educator with a doctorate degree, stagnant, feeling stuck in the front of the classroom. I was filled with confusion, resent, and disappointment. I'd concluded that my purpose in education must be something different than what I thought it was intended to be. I had become distracted by all I had not achieved and lost focus on, not only what was right in front of me, but also what I wanted my future to look like. Distractions will always get in the way, but I have learned that you cannot spend your time focusing on what has not yet been achieved. Distractions are simply small tests that are placed in your path to see how dedicated and passionate you are about what you do hope to achieve. This has been my experience.

I established my business in 2013. While I was networking and speaking at local events part time, the business was not flourishing on its own the way I'd hoped it would and I was not in a place professionally I had hoped to be by this time in my life. During the 2015-16 school year, this realization had become a large distraction in my life. I decided it was a good time to take a step back from the business to re-evaluate my purpose in some areas and gain clarity in others. I wasn't performing at my full potential due to stress and disappointment. I guess I figured it was a waste of time and no one really cared to notice anyway. I stopped writing because, in my mind, my words seemed to carry no value. I stopped asking for help or any guidance because I found so many people offered but very few ever came through. My life was at a professional stand still. My immediate family was all I had to hold me together during this setback. At least, that was my feeling at the time. It was a good time to reflect on my next steps.

During this time of reflection, I'd love to share that a miracle happened; that I got myself together, and my business began to flourish. Consequently, that was not the case at all. On the contrary, the business had taken an unexpected shift, but there were still so many other things that deterred my focus from growing it the way I had hoped.

I was a classroom teacher in an urban school setting at the time. I loved working with my scholars! I knew that working with them was my passion and my purpose. They were, quite obviously, one of the distractions hindering the growth and development of my business as well. It was quite difficult to provide my scholars with the quality education they *deserved* when I wasn't fully present to attend to their needs, but as long as I was compelled to be in the classroom, my scholars would receive all that I had to give. That was my duty and commitment. I was frequently reminded that these babies needed me, whether by a colleague or past scholar, and as much as I would have loved to be doing what I felt was my next step in professional growth, God spoke to me through them, reminding me that **at that moment** *they* needed me more than what I wanted for myself. It just wasn't my time. It was a distraction indeed, but because they meant so much to me and because I took pride in being a teacher leader, I welcomed it.

Another welcomed distraction I experienced during my time of reflection was the incredible privilege of working with some of the most amazing, knowledgeable, African American women educators, administrators, Ph.Ds, Ed.Ds, and nationally board certified teachers with whom I'd ever come in contact. Together, along with the most amazing project director, we led, facilitated, and mentored teachers across the country in building efficacy and culturally relevant ways to connect and teach to the urban school student. The opportunity to lead with this group of women facilitating professional development for teachers around the country was such a humbling experience. I was able to share my knowledge on a different level with educators from different avenues of life and had come to know that what I had to share was indeed valuable and made a significant contribution to their practice. I also had the opportunity to learn more about myself as a teacher leader and presenter, about teacher efficacy, and about what it looks like to step out on faith. This was exactly the opportunity I needed to help me shift the focus of my business and made me realize my skills were needed, just in a different capacity.

Well, you know what they say, for every positive, there is a negative. Why is it that with every positive experience, the negative ones seem to loom and linger the longest? Along my journey, I have received messages diminishing my professional worth. I've had my actions and words taken out of context in attempts to make me appear as if I were instigating a problem as opposed to navigating a solution. I have literally been looked at with scowls and grimaces for reasons I could not begin to explain. Each time, it left me disconcerted. Where had all of this come from? Just when these comments began to weigh heavy on my spirit and morale, I'd be reminded there would always be someone or something negative that would distract me from my goals and suppress the dreamer that was dwelling within me. What's more ironic was the fact that I *knew* better! Having had the opportunity to share many of my life experiences with young people and adults on what it means to live within your GREATNESS, I've shared the debilitating effects that negativity can bring to one's life. Negativity is all a part of the enemy's plan (earthly and spiritually) to incite one's demise. Staying focused is vital to successfully accomplishing one's goals, but beware! The distraction that is negativity is always lurking and ready to shift your focus at a moment's notice.

Here's the takeaway from my perception of negative and positive distractions. It is true that the good comes with the bad. The negative must coexist with the positive. This is a fact and there's really no way around it or controlling it. What can be controlled is how one reacts to such instances. My experience has found that negativity feeds and nourishes a fixed mindset. You will seemingly begin to believe the innuendos that are presented with every negative word and action. You'll find yourself wanting to give up on dreaming. When focused on positive people and things, you feed and grow your mind. You feel a sense of accomplishment and fulfillment and you will be pushed to challenge your own values and beliefs.

There are so many things that can distract you from what can be a life changing event. There are even times when you will find that you, yourself, can and will be your biggest distraction. In the end, you can choose to let negative distractions cloud your dreams or you can choose to allow the positive distractions make you stronger, keep you focused, and lead you to bigger and better opportunities. Stay focused on the bigger picture and use your distractions as stepping stones towards that something that is GREATER.

Reflection:

What distractions are you facing right now? What are some immediate changes you can make to help you get focused? Make a list and set some goals for your year.

_____

_____

_____

_____

_____

_____

_____

_____

_____

_____

_____

_____

_____

Chapter 10: Success

How exactly do you know you have achieved success in your career? Have you impacted the life of the children and families you served? Have you left your imprint in the field? I would spend many days asking myself these very questions. Where others may see a certain pay scale or title as success, educators seek much different affirmations. The growth, development, and academic achievement of our students are the greatest gifts of success an educator can receive. I have experienced this more and more in my teaching career and it has always filled me with so much joy that no amount of money could begin to compare.

It was days after Christmas in 2014 and the New Year was upon us. I had been thinking a lot about myself as a teacher and the many scholars I'd had the pleasure of teaching. I was at a crossroads in my life where I wondered if I was *really* making a difference. I could not remember a definitive moment when one of my scholars shared that I had truly impacted their lives. Perhaps I just hadn't noticed, but in that moment, I could not recall a scholar thanking me for all the work I had done for them. In fact, I probably received a few more side eyes and under the breath name calling, instead, and well, I suppose that was okay, too. I am passionate about all of them regardless of how they may have received it. Not to be disregarded, I did receive cute letters and nice pictures telling me how wonderful I was, but nothing that revealed a life changing epiphany for any of my scholars. I am not even sure what I was expecting at the time.

Ironically, something amazing and unexpected happened during this Christmas break. I was with my family making some Christmas gift exchanges, when I heard my name, "Mrs. Daugherty! Mrs. Daugherty!" I turned around to find this handsome young man walking up to me. I tried to distinguish his face, but I hadn't seen him since what I later learned was the fourth grade. This young man is now a young adult! He told me his name, "It's me. Justin!" (a pseudonym for confidentiality purposes) My eyes grew big and my heart filled with such joy! Not only did he recognize me, I was important enough to him that he stopped me to talk for a bit. He shared that he is now a senior at an out of state prep school. We talked for a moment and my heart filled with so much pride listening to all he had accomplished over the years.

He was always a bright young man and I knew he was destined for greatness, even in the fourth grade. I must admit, I would not have recognized him if he hadn't said anything to me first. I've taught hundreds of young people, in three different school systems. Names and faces tend to run together for me after so many years. But young Justin, I remembered. He was a scholar athlete being looked at by local colleges for the following year. He was another one that made it and was compelled enough to share his successes with me. Needless to say, after we went our separate ways, I couldn't stop smiling!

Later in the evening, I began to think to myself, "Who the heck was MY fourth-grade teacher?" For the life of me, I could not remember! I still can't, quite honestly. In fact, there are only a handful of teachers that I *do* remember. I remember them because they either said something that made me think, encouraged me, motivated me, or cared enough about me to sit me down and tell me to get myself together! These teachers helped mold my life. They helped me think about whom I was and who I wanted to become. They had fully *invested* in me and my future.

Here's my point. I know from experience how hard educators work. Day in and day out, you work to make a difference in the lives of learners. You write plans, you create, you grade, you analyze, and you work long, hard hours; more than anyone outside of the field cares to recognize. You demonstrate, encourage, motivate, and mediate. You watch over and protect, wipe tears and reassure. You empathize, realizing that some of your scholars have never received a caring touch or a kind word before you entered their lives. More often than not, they will leave us never disclosing the impact you've made on their lives. Know that you have, and you are, they just don't know how to communicate it to you.

After speaking with Justin, it dawned on me; *I* was one of the teachers Justin *remembered*. I had said something or done something to make him remember *me*. It is, in my opinion, the highest praise an educator can possibly receive. To be acknowledged by a young person you've taught and to hear of the wonderful things that are happening in his or her life is very fulfilling and gratifying. To hear that Justin made it against all odds and despite his circumstances because I said it was possible all those years ago, is the most priceless gift I could have received. Seeing Justin affirmed that I *was* succeeding!

The scripture says, "To whom much is given, much is required." Your purpose is to help your scholars see *beyond* their current circumstances. You have been charged with the task of steering them away from making poor choices which may lead them down the path of destruction, towards making better choices that will lead them to the path of their desired destiny. I'm here to tell you that this is **not** an easy task by any means and yes, you *will*, unfortunately, lose a few along the way, but not for lack of trying. Just keep in mind that there are many more *Justins* in your classrooms than not, who are waiting and wanting to learn how they too can make it. They may or may not tell you that you have affected their lives in any way, and really, that's okay. But, when that day comes, when you're walking along in the store and you hear your name being called by that one scholar, you too will receive the same gift that Justin afforded me on that very special day. When you are confronted in that moment, know that you have achieved success and you are doing it the best way you know how, one scholar at a time.

Reflection:

What does success look like to you? How do you know when you've succeeded? Is the journey toward success ongoing or is there a finite point when success is fully obtained? What next steps do you need to take in your journey?

_____

_____

_____

_____

_____

_____

_____

_____

_____

_____

_____

_____

_____

_____

Conclusion
Nothing Changes If Nothing Changes

November 4, 2013 was the day I published my first blog. After all the obstacles and discouragement I had received up to this point in my life, I recognized that I needed to take all the negative that had begun weighing me down and filling my soul with resentment and reconstruct it into something positive. I felt in my soul that my narrative, which chronicles my educational journey, could (and ultimately would) have a positive impact on educators and education. I had a story to tell and I wanted to share it in order to encourage, motivate, inspire, and empower other educators who also may have been struggling to define their GREATNESS.

It had been 8 months since I had successfully defended my doctoral study and 6 months since I had been conferred my doctoral degree in Teacher Leadership when I wrote that first blog. I was not in a good mental place. I had expected my degree to lead to greater opportunities in the field. That which I was expecting, had become a dream deferred. The longer I waited, the more opportunities passed me by, the angrier I became. Filled with self-pity, I began writing in a journal. My thoughts were coming so rapidly that I quickly began typing. Through all my venting, I reminded myself that everything happens for a reason; therefore, once I finished complaining, I challenged myself to address the lesson(s) that were learned from the issue or event. I'd found this to be so renewing that I took the chance of posting my prose on social media. I had no idea what to expect or how it would be received, but I felt that someone else needed to know they weren't alone and could find the lesson in their struggle as well.

Allow me to take you back to the months preceding the inception of my blog platform. As previously stated, after completing my degree, I had applied and interviewed for many positions. Rejection is ALWAYS difficult to deal with, but the one that was most upsetting for me was the one I received from the very district that helped me complete my doctoral degree. When I received the news that someone else had received the position for which I'd interviewed, I was crushed! Not because of who was chosen for the position, but because of who wasn't! I'd basically chalked it up to the fact that there must be something more for me to accomplish in the classroom, but I certainly didn't agree with nor had I accepted that fate set before me. As a result, I started the year filled with anger and resentment. I wanted no parts of anyone or anything. Everyone felt the disdain expelling from the air around me. My grade level team especially did, and unrightfully so. I had to release and regroup. So, in an effort to keep myself immersed in leadership roles, I chose to fill my plate with leadership opportunities. Listen, I thought it was a good idea at the time.

It probably took me until early October to end my itty-bitty pity party, or at least that's when I acknowledged I needed to get my head back in the game! It was during that time that I realized I *could* do what made me happy whether I was in a desired position or not. I just needed to be creative about the way in which I would reach other educators. This is when my blog was created and in January of 2014, with the support and encouragement of my husband, my family, and some great friends, the foundation was laid to establish **Transitions Educational Consulting, LLC**. If no one else would value my voice and my leadership abilities, I would value myself and learn to network and connect with others on my own terms. The mission would be to help students, teachers, and educational leaders define their personal and professional GREATNESS by teaching strategies I've learned and/or developed that engage, motivate, and promote leadership development. Maybe *this* was what I was meant to do. There was a problem though. While everything flowed so smoothly in my mind, I quickly found that developing a business was especially difficult while I continued to work in the classroom. There had to be a reason that I was still there **and** developing a business at the same time. God must have had a plan, right? I continued to trust the process and proceeded with taking on several roles in an effort to continue building capacity in leadership and development. In return, I would share my many experiences (highs and lows), my lessons, and my reflections with other educators across the nation. At the risk of exposing my imperfections, flaws, successes, and/or celebrations, I became very transparent, in every conceivable way, in order to help other educators, like myself, grow. I have to say, the blog turned out to be a major high point of that school year. It had been received and appreciated far and wide by so many, serving its intended purpose of encouraging, inspiring, supporting, and empowering educators from all over the country. The blog had suddenly become my platform to promote and advocate for changes in teachers' instructional practices. Through my own experiences, I found that there was a gap between teachers' instruction and student learning, but I also found that educators have become skilled at masking their incompetencies and flaws with educational jargon and dog and pony shows, thus impeding students academic growth, widening the achievement gap, and contributing to the educational disparities that already exist in our systems. It was time for change, and I was committed to finding ways to help bridge the gap for learners everywhere.

As with years before, this year was no different than any other filled with vicissitudes. I'd made great strides and endured some intense disappointments as well. I'd been told I was unsupportive on the low end and awe inspiring on the high end. I'd heard that I take things personally and am sensitive, but also had been acknowledged for my strength, courage, and reflective insight. I had even been told that the completion of my doctoral degree would elicit appreciation from some, while others would depreciate it by refusing to address me as Dr. Daugherty. I had, admittedly, let a few colleagues down with poorly thought out decisions, but had lifted and motivated SO MANY more with my intentionality and connectedness to others! I had experienced a whirlwind of emotions and changes, but this is all a necessary part of what healthy, effective change looks like.

As with everything, I learned a few things along the way. I cannot even begin to share the number of applications I had submitted, the number of interviews, and the number of rejections I'd received that year as I worked to find my niche. There had been many, MANY *jobs* that passed me by. In hindsight, this turned out to be a blessing for the mere fact that they were JOBS! This is important to clarify. A job is a noun, a *thing*. A job is defined by the qualifications someone else determines and is subject to change based on someone else's needs at that time. Let me be clear in saying that this is *my* perception, *my* personal reflection, *my* personal experience with *jobs*. A job may or may *not* align with one's long-term goals or passion, especially on paper, but because other people determine what "the job" is, there seems no certainty that one will ever truly be a good fit for "the job". In my reflection, this presented as a profound realization for me. It was not a *job* I was looking for, but space to promote and impact change; unapologetically, passionately, and transparently. Through it all, I learned that even though I have made mistakes, I am not lacking in knowledge, value, or worth. In my opinion, sitting within your vulnerabilities is what allows you to better see the changes necessary to strengthen your practice.

Lastly, I acknowledge that change is ALWAYS occurring and indeed, change is difficult. Along this journey, **my** journey toward GREATNESS, I have learned so much about myself as a person and as a professional. I no longer allow jobs to define my future. I have committed to continuing to create my own opportunities and accept that I AM the creator of my own destiny. Of course, I will make adjustments where necessary and changes when needed as I continue on the path that has been set before me. I have come to realize that with each new day, with every person's shared perception, that nothing will change, if nothing changes.

As I close, I would like for you to consider the following questions. What will you do to impact change in your school community or district? Are you doing your part to bridge the gap? What does your journey to GREATNESS look like? As you work to define your personal and professional GREATNESS, commit to demonstrating what this will look like in your classrooms and community. Your defined

GREATNESS is what will keep you grounded in your values and morals and act as guiding principles as you continue to grow and develop in your personal and professional life. Your definition may differ from the characteristics in this book or you may choose to adopt the characteristics outlined here. Whichever definition you choose to embrace, you must work persistently and dedicate yourself daily to instilling them into your everyday life. Once you have clearly defined these important aspects, they will help you keep your steps ordered and your life prioritized. Will you get off track? Of course you will. With a clearly defined path, you will have a more positive outlook and infallible direction along your journey to success. Your GREATNESS defined is your destiny. Take control of your life's journey. Take your GREATNESS and allow it to mold you so that you can make a difference and leave your unique imprint on the world.

References

Allington, R. (2011) What at risk readers need. *Educational Leadership, 68* (6), 40-45.

Bandura, A. (1993). Perceived self-efficacy in cognitive development and functioning. *Educational Psychologist, 28*(2), 117-148.

Bandura, A. (1997). Behavior theory and the models of man (1974). In J. M. Notterman (Ed.), *The evolution of psychology: Fifty years of the American Psychologist (pp. 154–172)*. Washington, DC: American Psychological Association.

Bandura, A. (2008). An agentic perspective on positive psychology. In S. J. Lopez (Ed.), Praeger perspectives. *Positive psychology: Exploring the best in people (Vol. 1., pp. 167–196)*. Westport, CT: Praeger Publishers/Greenwood Publishing Group.

Daugherty, K. B. & Little, M. (2016). Teacher efficacy and implications for teaching our underserved students. *PHILLIS: Journal for Research on African American Women, 4*(1), 44-49.

Dweck, C. (2008). *Mindset: The new psychology of success.* New York: Ballantine Books.

Dweck, C. (2014, November). *The power of believing that you can improve.* [Video file]. Retrieved from https://www.ted.com/talks/carol_dweck_the_power_of_believing_that_you_can_improve?utm_campaign=tedspread&utm_medium=referral&utm_source=tedcomshare

Kabat-Zinn, J. (2003) Mindfulness-based stress reduction (MBSR). *Constructivism in the Human Sciences, 8*(2), 2003, 73-107.

Moorehead, J. (2012, June 19). Stanford University's **Carol Dweck** on the growth mindset and education. *OneDublin.org: Celebrating education excellence.* Retrieved from https://onedublin.org/2012/06/19/stanford-universitys-carol-dweck-on-the-growth-mindset-and-education/

Protheroe, N. (2008). Teacher efficacy: What is it and does it matter? *Principal, 87*(5), 42-45.

Tschannen-Moran, M., Woolfolk Hoy, A., & Hoy, W. K. (1998). Teacher efficacy: Its meaning and measure. *Review of Educational Research, 68,* 202-248.

Tschannen-Moran, M. & Woolfolk Hoy, A. (2001). Teacher efficacy: Capturing an elusive construct. *Teaching and Teacher Education, 17,* 783-805.

www.ingramcontent.com/pod-product-compliance
Lightning Source LLC
Chambersburg PA
CBHW051948160426
43198CB00013B/2347